C000272022
Love & Best Wishes
Alan Robson
Night Owls
Metro + Tees

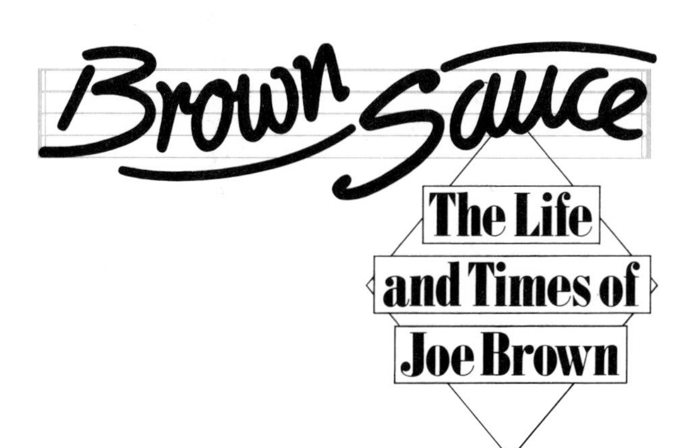
Brown Sauce
The Life
and Times of
Joe Brown

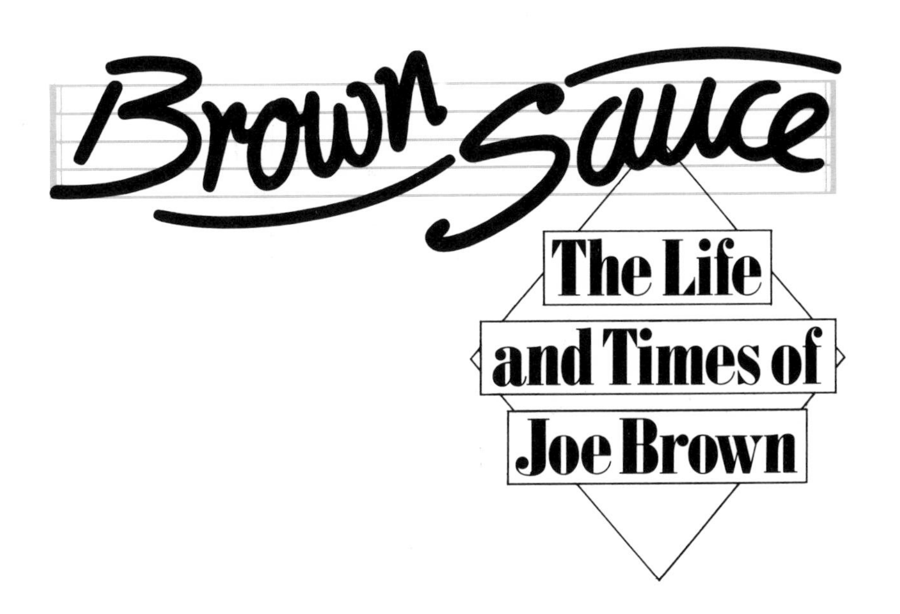

with
Graeme Wright

Foreword by
George Harrison

Willow Books
Collins
8 Grafton Street, London W1X 3LA
1986

Willow Books
William Collins Sons & Co Ltd
London · Glasgow · Sydney
Auckland · Toronto · Johannesburg

First published in Great Britain 1986

British Library Cataloguing in Publication Data
Brown, Joe
Brown sauce.
I. Title
828′.91409 PR6052.R613/

ISBN 0 00 218160 6

Filmset by Ace Filmsetting Ltd, Frome, Somerset
Printed in Great Britain by Mackays of Chatham Ltd

Contents

Acknowledgements
Pages 15, 55 Reveille Newspapers Ltd; 25, 47 Terry; 39 Rex Features Ltd; 42 London Weekend Television Ltd; 51 D. C. Thomson & Co. Ltd; 52 Worrall's Photographic Press Service; 77 Peter Johnson; 120 *News Chronicle/Daily Dispatch* (Manchester); 130 Lensmen International; 138 North Thames Gas Board/Roy Keirby; 140 *Daily Express*; 179, 221 Scope Features/Brian Moody; 214 RAF Official Crown Copyright; 222 Mick Gregory.

Foreword by George Harrison

For me, Joe has always been a guitar player first, and all the rest (which there is quite a lot of . . .) has been secondary. I suppose that's because back in the olden days as a teenager watching all his TV shows I was suitably impressed with his crew cut and Gibson 335, not to mention his cheeky sense of humour and the fact that he was the biggest nudger in Larry Parnes' camp!

Although Joe can act and entertain (in the showbiz sense) on many difficult stages (including his Academy-award-winning Christmas TV commercials for Woolworths), I must say he appears to me at his happiest as a musician, playing the guitar, mandolin, banjo, harmonica and fiddle, and composing songs (he's a clever little bastard!). It is my pleasure to know him mostly on that level, though I would add that he is also not bad with an old joke or two or three, as you are about to find out when you turn this page . . .

February 1986

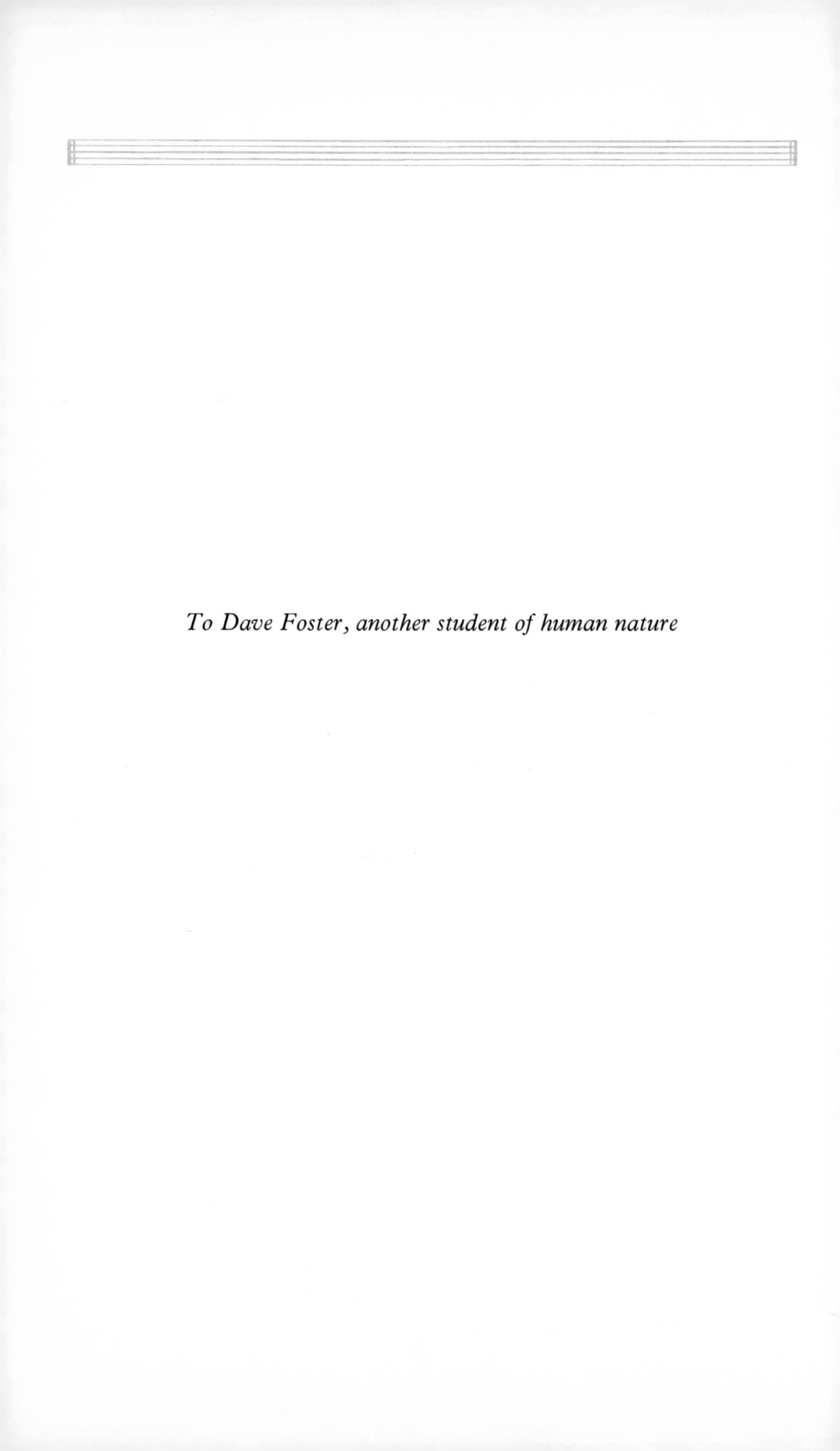

To Dave Foster, another student of human nature

Introduction

I wouldn't say *Brown Sauce* is an autobiography as such. True, it's about me, but it's just as much about the people, the characters, I've met during my life. People like the Uncle Harrys of this world who scream jokes at you after funerals, excusing themselves with 'Take my word for it. If Eric was alive now, instead of going up in smoke like wot 'e did twenty minutes ago, 'e'd turn in 'is grave – if 'e 'ad one – to see all you miserable bleeders 'ere. Come on everyone. 'Ow about a song?'

There's a stony silence during which Harry draws breath. Then 'Tie a yellow ribbon rahnd the old oak tree.'

People tend to show their emotions differently, and with the Uncle Harrys it's just their way. A pain in the neck, really, but understandable none the less.

The book started, I suppose, because of Wee Georgie Wood, whom I first met when I was initiated into the show business charity, the Grand Order of Water Rats. A very sharp, witty little bloke, he wasn't always liked by everyone, but Georgie and I hit it off straight away. Now, as well as being in the Water Rats, Georgie was also a member of the Savage Club, and he invited me along to one of their evenings. What he didn't tell me was that my name would be on the list to do a little 'something' during the evening – and by the time I discovered this it was too late to do anything about it.

To be honest, when the bloke stood up and said to all the eminent gentlemen in the room, 'Now, here he is, Joe Brown!' I still didn't know what I was going to do. So I started telling them stories about myself when I was a kid, and about me mum when we lived in a pub in the East End, and somehow it worked. They roared their heads off, and afterwards one bloke, who was an author, told me I should write all the stories down.

When I'd written a few I showed them to George Harrison, who also thought they were a good laugh and put me in touch with his publishers. But while they were very helpful, they weren't really pushing me, and I'm the sort of person who needs to be pushed. I need a deadline.

That *Brown Sauce* came to be a book was more coincidence than anything else. It was the day of a London Underground strike, and I'd been in London having tea at the Ritz – having tea at the Ritz with Joe Brown was a prize in a competition. (I ended up with a schoolteacher and a policeman.) As luck would have it, when I went outside it was raining cats and dogs and it was impossible to get a cab anywhere. So I started walking.

'Hello, Joe!' said a bloke in the car salesroom in Berkeley Square as I walked past. 'What're you doing walking in the rain? You're getting soaking wet.'

'I'm trying to get to Paddington,' I said. 'I can't get a taxi anywhere.'

'Tell you what,' he said. 'I'll be finished here in twenty minutes. I'll run you round there.'

'That's very nice of you, mate. Thanks very much. I'll just go round to the pub and have a drink.'

Anyway, while I'm standing in the pub, nursing my gin and tonic, some other bloke yells across to his mates, 'If you two want a ride to Paddington, you'd better hurry up.'

Well, that pricked my ears up.

''Scuse me, mate,' I said. 'Did I hear you say you were going to Paddington? Don't fancy giving me a lift, do you?'

He looked at me a bit funny like, then he recognized me and said he would. Pity about the bloke from the car salesroom, I thought, but here was a car waiting outside the pub, so I piled in the back with these other blokes.

'Isn't it time you wrote a book?' asked the driver when we got going.

'Funny you should say that,' I answered, 'because I'm trying to write one at the moment.'

I could see them all looking at each other.

'Why?' I asked. 'Who are you?'

'We're from Collins, the publishers,' one of them replied. 'Why don't you come in and talk to us? Here, I'll give you my card.'

'Funny thing, that,' I said to Vicki, my wife, when I got home and told her the story. You should phone him, she said, but before doing that I thought I should clear it first with George's mate, Brian Roylance.

He was very good about it so I phoned Collins, and next thing I knew I had a contract and an advance. Which was the best thing that could have happened, because now I had to do it. I was on a deadline and I had their money.

So that's how *Brown Sauce* came about. I'd like to thank George Harrison for his enthusiasm and Brian Roylance for his initial encouragement and help; and also Alan Smith and Caroline White at Collins Willow for having faith in the potential of the stories, and for being patient while Graeme and I got our act and this book together.

1 Winkles on the weekend

I was sitting sorting small change from shrimps' heads and empty winkle shells. It was two minutes past one and Billy Cotton had just shattered the Sunday peace with a particularly raucous 'Wakey, wakey!' Lord knows what time he got up in the morning. Me, I'd just finished the winkle round, having started at five-thirty that morning and pushed a barrow fifteen miles around the East End of London. Now it was ten minutes off and then back up the Barking Road to Poplar with a four-wheeled jellied eel stall. With a bit of luck I might be home by two o'clock on Monday morning with fifteen bob clear profit for the weekend and time for some kip before another week of school. Oh, the joys of being your own boss at the age of thirteen! Some people were still in bed. They didn't know what they were missing.

I got into the jellied eel business as a result of a good line I was doing in energy supply. I ran an extension lead from the light socket in my bedroom down to the light on Lenny Bristow's eel stall which stood on the bomb site beside my Uncle Joe's pub in Plaistow. As I was getting paid ten bob a day for this and Uncle Joe was paying the electricity bill, it was a useful little earner. However, I was filled with the ambition of youth (not to mention being worried about what would happen if Uncle Joe ever discovered where his electricity was going), so when Lenny asked me if I'd like to help him out, it was too good a chance to miss. Besides, Lenny was practically family. His Aunt Edie was my Uncle Joe's girlfriend. Deaf as a post, she was, and all of sixty-five. I caught them at it one day: walked into the bedroom and there was Uncle Joe, all twenty stone of him, sitting on the bed with his nightshirt up over his fat thighs and Edie on her knees in front of him – cutting his toenails! I reckon they got Lenny to give me a job so I'd spend my weekends pushing barrows and stalls around Plaistow and Poplar and Uncle Joe could get his other foot done.

To be honest about it, I didn't know what I was letting myself in for. We'd start off on Saturday morning, like I said, about half past five, hire a barrow for a bob, and fill a big tin bath full of winkles, brown shrimps, pink shrimps, whelks and all the usual kinds of shellfish. Then off we'd go, west up the Barking Road as far as Canning Town bridge, down Silvertown way and then back to the bridge to work our way round Poplar. We'd reckon on being home in Plaistow by a quarter to one.

In the afternoon Lenny pulled and I pushed a four-wheeled eel stall that was built to be drawn by a horse back up the Barking Road and over the bridge and set it up outside a pub in the Aberfeldy Road, about a mile up from the Blackwall Tunnel, which is a hole in the ground just across from the Isle of Dogs. You hear about it on the radio most days: the tunnel, that is, not the pub. It's one of those places where cars like to break down and lorries shed their loads. The pub, which was called the Aberfeldy, has never been mentioned on the radio that I know of, but that didn't stop us staying outside it till closing time on Saturday night, whereupon we'd take the stall all the way back to Plaistow. Sunday was just the same.

The first weekend we were out, I remember it as if it was yesterday. We were pulling and pushing the eel stall back over Canning Town bridge and I was thinking that once we got to the brow it would be downhill all the way to Plaistow. When we reached the brow we paused for a breather and Lenny, leaning back in the traces, said to me, 'If we've done well, there'll be a little brown note in it for you, mate.' And I thought to myself, ten bloody bob for a weekend's work! No wonder they called him the Robin Hood of the East End. I'd been better off supplying him with electricity.

He was good with the old folk though, Lenny. I can still see the pensioners coming out from their houses with a pint mug of empty winkle shells hidden under their aprons. If Lenny knew they were on hard times, he'd tip the empty shells into our bath of full winkles, mix them all up, and then spoon a pint back into the pensioner's mug – and only charge them for half a pint. It was Lenny's opinion that there were always other people who could afford to pay for a pint, even if it did contain some empty shells. There was one old girl in Silvertown who wouldn't hand over her empty shells until we'd given her a pint of fresh winkles. She must've thought they were worth something. Like the empty bottles she took back to the pub.

Me outside The Sultan in Plaistow.

One Saturday I tried doing a round on my own, only Lenny caught me. I came round this corner with a barrow full of gear, shouting 'All fresh winkles' at the top of my voice, and there was Lenny on the other side of the road. I stopped 'All fresh winkling' in a twinkling, I can tell you, but I knew from the sound of running feet and the 'What d'you think you're up to?' coming from behind me that he'd seen me. Oh-oh, I thought, I'm for it now, because Lenny wasn't the sort you stood about and argued with. He had a name around our way as a useful welterweight; southpaw. It was said he could box a bit as well. Mind you, my mum knew how to use her fists and all, but she was in a different class from Lenny – heavyweight! And the only Marquess of Queensberry she'd heard of was a pub off the Barking Road.

2 Early days

One of my earliest recollections of Mum was that the first three fingers of her left hand were always bandaged. I used to ask why, being a loving son and all that, but she wouldn't let on. So I reckoned it was to save her knuckles from bruising when she poleaxed the local drunks in the bar. Henry Cooper had nothing on my mum. Six foot squat, someone once described her: like a butch John Wayne. A drunk once made a pass at her – I mean, he'd have to have been drunk – and next thing he knew he was flying through the plate-glass window. He wasn't the only one either. Mum reckoned it wasn't worth good working time having to open the door before throwing the drunks out on the street. She must've cost Charrington's a fortune in plate glass. I don't think the putty in that window ever got hard.

There were six of us living in that pub: my mum and dad, my younger brother Pete and me, and Uncle Joe and his son John. The Sultan, the pub was called, in Grange Road, Plaistow, and Uncle Joe was the landlord; which meant my mum did all the work. Cooking, cleaning, barmaid, bouncer: you name it, she got lumbered with it. And she had a sick husband to look after. Almost as long as I can remember, Dad was in bed or in hospital.

In fact, it was because of him she had those three bandaged fingers. When he went to bed at night, he'd put a sprung mousetrap in his trouser pocket, and if Mum was on the dip for his loose change – wham! He'd just open one eye, grin, turn over and chuckle himself to sleep, the mean old sod.

Mum took it all in her stride, though, and somehow she managed to keep going. However, she did draw the line at his teeth. If there was

Me, Mum and my younger brother Pete with our dog Trixie which used to entertain pub customers.

one thing she was repulsed by – maybe even frightened of – it was anything false: false teeth, wigs, wooden legs, politicians. To her dying day she had just one tooth hanging down from her jaw rather than have false teeth. When she grinned you thought you were looking at the back end of a JCB.

The time I'm talking about with the teeth followed one of my father's long stints in hospital. Once he was in there, and unbeknown to Mum, he'd asked if something could be done about his teeth while he was

Dad keeping his mouth shut so his teeth don't show.

under the anaesthetic. When he came home, he walked into our back room and spluttered, 'Look, Rene.' Whereupon he opened his mouth to reveal a huge set of ill-fitting yellowish National Health choppers made of some sort of plastic. Mum screamed in terror and, leaping up, ripped the teeth from his mouth and threw them on to the fire – where they disappeared in a sheet of blue flame.

'Ot idoo goo bat poor?' he cried.

'You're not wearing those bleeding things!' she said. 'They're bad enough with your face wrapped round 'em, but I ain't waking up in the morning with them grinning at me from a glass of water.'

From that day on the old man got thinner and thinner. Probably because of his illness, plus a touch of starvation. He died when I was twelve, and all he left Mum was the suit he stood up in, with the mousetrap still in the trouser pocket. She buried him in it. Mousetrap and all.

To be honest, I don't know how Mum managed in those days, though I guess she was used to it. She always had a good sense of humour, and that was probably worth more to her than money in the bank. When my father was a child, she used to tell us, his family were so poor they couldn't afford to buy him any clothes. He wasn't even allowed out in the street to play with the other kids because he had nothing to wear.

Then when he was eighteen things got better. His dad bought him a cap so he could have a look out of the window!

With that sort of poverty in the family it wasn't surprising I was always on the lookout for ways of making a few bob. My mate Dennis – 'Pepper' my mother called him because after he'd had nits and his head had been shaved his hair growing again made the top of his head look like a pepper pot – well, Dennis and I made a good team when it came to making money. One way was the empty bottle fiddle. I used to pass the empty bottles over the wall at the back of the pub and Dennis would take them round the front to collect the money on them. It wasn't so much robbing my family as a redistribution of wealth, with a small handling charge for Dennis. Just like VAT when you come to think of it.

And there was always totting – scrap metal, copper wire, junk and so forth: quite a lucrative business with brass at one and a tanner a pound, especially if you slung a couple of bricks in the bag. I'm sure Georgie Dance, the bloke who weighed it, knew what the game was but he never said anything.

Since there were quite a lot of bomb sites in our area, there was always something lying around. Dennis and I found a couple of hundred-weight of lead once, lying around on the church roof. I think the vicar was grateful we took that, because, as Dennis pointed out, 'Now he won't have to fill up his font when it's raining.' Always ready to do someone a good turn were Dennis and me.

Not everyone appreciated us, though. Uncle Joe went blue in the face when he discovered we'd nicked the brass beer taps from the Sultan's cellar, and Mum had to go down to Tommy Hoadley's scrap yard to get them back. But Tommy was a nice man. He handed them over without even asking for his money back: the money he'd paid Dennis and me earlier in the day when we took them in. Years later, after I'd made a bit of a name for myself, I went back to see Tommy, just to say hello and thanks, like. He was still the same, and so was his yard. The little hut he called his office was just inside the gate, and Georgie Dance was still working there, sorting out the bricks from the scrap, no doubt. We talked over old times for a while, then as I was making a move to leave he went to his desk, unlocked a drawer and pulled out a little canvas bag. It was full of gold sovereigns and he gave me two of them. 'For the kids,' he said. He was good like that, Tommy.

That's how it used to be, though. People were kind to those who didn't have anything. My mum was the same with neighbours who came into the jug and bottle bar to have their jugs and bottles filled with beer. They'd hand over a ten-bob note, say, and if Mum knew they were on hard times she'd give them change for a quid. 'Bless you, Rene,' I'd hear them say, which I thought was a bit strong when all she'd done was fill their jug with a drop of draught ale. I suppose she thought Uncle Joe could afford a little charity now and then.

She wasn't so charitable towards the prostitute, however. Dennis and I used to watch her at it sometimes in the bombed-out house next to the pub – until Mum got to hear what was going on and there was hell to pay. She and a couple of her mates stormed in there one evening like commandos on a raid and next thing you know there's this little bloke belting down the road trying to pull his trousers up. The woman never worked our road again, I can tell you that.

Not that there'd have been anywhere for her to take her clients after Dennis and I had finished with the pair of bombed-out houses. They'd been standing derelict for years, and one day we heard that the brewery were sending a demolition team round to knock them down. By the time they arrived we'd done the job for them.

A masterpiece of primitive engineering it was: a cross between Attila the Hun and a howitzer. Let me set the scene. Running behind the pub and the houses was what was grandly called the Northern Outfall – what most of us would call a sewer. It was covered over, of course, which made a nice grassy bank for us kids to play on. Every so often there were concrete-lined shafts – for ventilation, I suppose – and down one of these we put a couple of lengths of timber with a tyre tube strung between them. It was an instant catapult. Put a brick or lump of concrete in the rubber tube, fire it and it brought down a bit of wall just as well as any ball and chain on a crane. Cheaper too. Only it wasn't so accurate. One missile went straight between the pub and the houses, flew across the street and smashed down the front door of a house opposite. Industrial accident, I believe it's called these days.

But then we never did get on well with that family. Ever since the time their son broke my brother Pete's nose in a fight. Pete was only ten at the time; this other kid was fourteen and a real bully. Spoilt too, being the only boy in a family of six much older sisters, all of them hard nuts. I wasn't much more than eleven myself, but that didn't stop Pete threatening to set me on to this other kid. Mind you, I did my best to ignore the challenge, and it wasn't my fault this kid came looking for me when I was playing baseball – and batting.

That night, after his mum and sisters had brought him home from the dental hospital, they came looking for Mum. The whole street knew they were coming and so did my mother. She was waiting for them with a milk bottle full of sand. Talk about the gunfight at the OK corral! It was *High Noon*, *The Wild Bunch* and *Amazon Woman Meets the Monsters from Outer Space* on a triple-bill. The neighbours hadn't seen anything like it since the Blitz.

Mum laid out the lot of them and never even broke the bottle. Sheer poetry.

3 An apple, an orange and an 'alf-a-crown

I'd gone down to Southend to do a gig for a mate of mine. You could say it was a favour because I never got paid for it, but then that seems to be the way of the world these days. It must've been summer because I remember it was raining monkeys, with an east wind howling off the North Sea like a pack of wolves after a tough old granny. Two old dears were making their way to a fancy dress party done up as Scott of the Antarctic, and the only place with any sign of light or life was a caff. Inside was an old fellow wiping the counter with a dirty dishcloth, so I made his afternoon by ordering a cup of tea and a bacon sandwich.

'I used to come down here when I was a kid,' I told him, just to be conversational. 'On pub outings from Plaistow.'

He looked at me across the counter and smiled at a memory.

'Apple, a norange and an 'alf-a-crown, eh?'

'Yeah, that's it,' I laughed with him. 'Here or Walton-on-the-Naze. One or the other it was always the same. Off the charabanc into a big tent for your dinner, and on the way out you all lined up for your apple, orange and half-a-crown. Something to keep you going and your spending money for the afternoon.'

'You don't 'ave to tell me, son,' he said. 'I remember it well. Little bleeders running all about the place nicking stuff out of the shops while their folks sat in the pub from opening time to closing time.'

'Right, mate,' I laughed. 'And on the way home we'd stop at every pub as well. I reckon they planned it so we'd get here when the pubs opened and we'd leave just in time to catch them opening on the way home. All except the poor bloody driver. He was too scared to leave his coach in case we took it apart while he was in the pub.'

Funny how something like that brings back memories. Like mentioning pub outings to the old boy in the caff and his immediate thought was of the apple, orange and half-crown every kid was given on his local pub's outing. It was all part of the old East End tradition. But if anyone had mentioned pub outings to me, I'd have thought of two other things: galvanized buckets and mouldies.

At the Sultan there were three outings. One for the men, one for the women and one for the kids. About the only thing they had in common was that there'd be singing all the way to the seaside and all the way home. I once got lumbered with playing the guitar with Georgie Dance on the women's outing, and that taught me a thing or two, I can tell you. The language and the behaviour of the women when they were away from their menfolk had to be heard and seen to be believed. I remember Georgie saying to me on the way back, 'There's only one thing worse than a coach load of pissed women – and that's two coach loads!'

But more memorable than the outings themselves was the excitement that surrounded the departure – especially on the men's outing. First of all the charabanc would pull up outside the pub early in the morning and the men would begin loading all that was needed for the mammoth thirty-mile journey to Walton-on-the-Naze. Crates and crates of light ale, brown ale, stout, dozens of packets of crisps – plus three or four galvanized buckets for the patrons who couldn't hold on till the next stop. Then, after a lot of running around and messengers being sent to hurry along the latecomers, all the men would sit in the charabanc in readiness for the off.

Suddenly, up would go the cry from us kids:

'CHUCK OUT YER MOULDIES!'

And as one, down would go the windows of the coach and the men would throw out all their loose change.

What a scramble! Kids everywhere, fighting in the street for pennies, halfpennies and, if you were lucky, threepenny bits. Me and Dennis always tried to get near Ted Mead's window because with Ted it was always half-crowns. Good old Ted!

Not that we ever called him Ted in those days. He was always Mr Mead to us kids, and that was a real sign of respect. More so when you consider that he was the local bookie. Yet he was the only mister I knew when I was a kid. The schoolteachers were always sir – to their faces. There was something of the gent about Ted though. Middle-aged, always in a light grey suit and trilby hat, he looked more like a toff than a bookie: like one of those Englishmen who've spent much of their life in the Far East instead of all of it in the East End. Ted Heath – the politician, not the bandleader – reminded me of Ted a bit. Or could it have been that Ted Heath reminded me of a bookie?

I suppose you could say that Ted (Mead, not Heath) was a self-made man. The trouble was he can't have made his legs long enough because he was always getting caught by the Old Bill. You'd hear a commotion in the street and there would be Ted, hoofing it as fast as he could, throwing betting slips away with one hand to lose the evidence and half-crowns with the other hand to lighten his load, his little legs going up and down getting him nowhere. And all the time the local copper was getting closer and closer.

Me and Dennis used to make a few bob as bookie's runners for Ted – until we got caught red-handed with the betting slips on us. Luckily the sergeant let us off with a good talking to and a message for Ted.

'Two bob each way on the winner in the free-firty at Firff!'

People like Ted were an essential part of the community in the East End. There'd be the corner shop, the pub and there'd be the bookie. He was like a local tradesman. There was a time when Ted was ill and the whole neighbourhood was talking about it. He was that popular – and he was generous too. If you were in trouble with the rent or the gas, it was always Ted you went to, and he took a personal pride in being able to help you out. It was almost as if it was a family matter to him. In a way I suppose people like Ted were overtaken by the betting shop and

Me (third from the left) aged about eight, dressed as a sultan for the street fancy dress party. Mum made my costume.

the welfare state: just as the local community spirit went up in smoke with the high-rise flats. More's the pity. I don't suppose they chuck out their mouldies any more either.

Yet it wasn't so long ago that it was a ritual observed by everyone on the day of the pub outing. Nobody would toss out a farthing until they were ready to go. Then, on the word, it would all just happen. Down would go the windows, out would come the mouldies, Georgie and Arthur Dance would strike up a song and the charabanc would trundle off, leaving us kids trying to get the gratings up in the gutters, just in case any money had rolled through them. (Fat chance with me and Dennis around.)

I remember great street parties, too, when the Dances used to drag their old piano out on to the pavement and the whole street had a knees-up. Great days – when streets were horizontal as opposed to vertical. Imagine your mum telling you to 'Pop upstairs but one to borrow a cup of sugar.' It doesn't sound right somehow.

You never see people on the street the way you used to, either. Back then it seemed that they were always there: kids during the day; the men after closing time, usually gathered round the local lamp-post singing drunken songs while Georgie Dance played his guitar with a matchstick for a plectrum.

Because he could play the guitar, Georgie was my local hero, and when I was twelve I bought an old guitar from him for a quid. Tall and

One of my first guitars.

thin, with protruding teeth and a cleft palate that did nothing for his renditions of 'The Tenneffee Walff', he was one of a large family, all of whom wore knotted neckerchiefs and played some musical instrument. One played the piano accordion and another the piano. But what made them even more important was that they were the only family in the neighbourhood with their own telephone. We didn't even have one and we were in the pub. You always knew when things were getting out of hand in the bar when you heard Uncle Joe shout through to my mum: 'Rene, go round to Rene Dance's and phone the police.' If that didn't quieten them, Mum would emerge from the kitchen with her milk bottle full of sand and next day the man from the brewery would be around to replace the window.

Harry Young, the pub's piss artist, was one of those who went through the window. It was the only time in living memory I can recall him not being in the pub during opening hours. He had a 'wall eye', Harry: it looked straight ahead while the good eye swivelled through 180 degrees to see what was going on. That probably accounted for the way he always wore his cap at a crooked angle over the 'wall eye'.

Poor old Harry. I can picture him now. All done up for a pint and a singsong down at the Sultan. A great lad for the singing was Harry. He'd be standing in front of his mirror, admiring himself, and the last thing he does before leaving the house is put on his cap. Looks at himself again. Flicks the peak to what he thinks is a rakish, jaunty angle, rubs his hands in satisfaction at his appearance and sets off for the pub chuckling at the effect. In his mind's eye, a regular Jack the lad. In the public's eye, a cap going west on a face going east.

And his singing!

Me mum said he sounded like a wounded wolf – and she had to listen to him every night. Because every night the regulars would get him up to do a solo.

'No, no,' he'd say, all mock modesty. 'Not tonight.'

'C'mon 'Arry,' they'd say, egging him on. 'Give us a song. Give us "Please release me".'

Once, twice, thrice.

'No, no, I can't. Not tonight.'

'Course you can, 'Arry. Just one song.'

'All right then, lads. Just one song.'

You knew he would. He knew he would. And it was awful. Every night it was awful. What made it worse, what made it funnier, was that he always sang the wrong words. And the other buggers would be sniggering into their pints, taking the mickey out of him as he howled:

'Please delete me, let me go', no doubt hoping that Uncle Joe would wipe his slate clean. Or it might be 'Love letters down the Strand'. Every one a winner.

As for Uncle Joe wiping anyone's slate clean, there was no chance. Uncle Joe was as tight as they come where money was concerned. During the war, if there wasn't time to grab the cash from the till and get to the air raid shelter before the bombs fell, he'd put his head under the till and wrap his big mutton arms over the top of it. Mum reckoned his philosophy was 'If the till goes up, I'm going with it'. Still, it did mean everyone else could get into the shelter at the bottom of the garden at the back of the pub. Usually it was a case of Uncle Joe and the cash first, women and children second – or not at all as almost happened one night. All twenty stone of Uncle Joe got stuck fast in the entrance with Mum, my baby brother Pete in her arms, me and Dad and all the neighbours lining up behind him waiting to get in while somewhere up above we could hear the drone of the bombers getting closer. No amount of pulling and tugging would move him, so in the end Mum took matters into her own hands and planted her right foot up his backside. Uncle Joe shot forward like a drowning whale. Don't ask me how they got him out again.

Uncle Joe was my father's brother, and originally they came from the Midlands, which is where my Uncle Ern had a farm. They were a big family on account of their mother having married twice and produced eighteen kids. Her first husband was a bloke called Brown, the second a bloke called Gray. Every man named White, Black or Green had skipped the county before she could get round to them. Anyway, the Browns were farmers and the Grays were publicans, but Gran mixed them up a bit, and by the time she'd finished there were Browns in pubs and Grays on the land. Come Christmas those in the pubs would take bottles of whisky and gin to the farms and come away with chickens and turkeys and sausages for the festivities.

Come the school holidays it'd be me and various cousins making our way to Melton Mowbray to work for Uncle Ern. Ten bob a week he paid us, and we put in the same hours as the farm workers. Hoeing, harvesting and haymaking from dawn to dusk, and if you were lucky you got ten minutes driving the tractor.

As well as the farm, Uncle Ern ran a book at the local racecourse, and it wasn't unusual for the punters to come up to the farm at night to place their bets. There was one bloke, though, that Uncle Ern didn't take to at all: maybe he suspected him of being a copper's nark. So one evening Uncle Ern and my dad, who was up at the farm for the summer,

The Lincolnshire poachers – early members of the Brown family.

set him up. When they saw him coming Uncle Ern went out of the kitchen, leaving Dad in there to talk to him. As he always did, the bloke started going on about how hard up he was, and after a couple of minutes of this, Dad took a pat of butter from the larder, wrapped some paper round it and handed it to him.

''Ere you are,' he said, all conspiratorial like. 'Don't tell Ern I've given it to you. If you 'ear 'im coming, stick it under your 'at,' which the bloke was still wearing, despite being in the house. Out in the passage, of course, Uncle Ern has been listening to all this, and pretty soon he makes a bit of a noise, gives the bloke time to slip the butter under his hat, and comes in full of the joys of life, telling the bloke what a pleasure it is to see him, asking about his family, discussing the best bets for the next meeting. At first the bloke wouldn't stop talking, but it was a warm summer evening and there was a coal range baking bread in the kitchen. Pretty soon there were trickles of butter making their way down his face, through his hair and under his collar. Uncle Ern and my dad could contain themselves no longer. They burst out laughing, and the sound followed the man all the way across the yard as he stomped to the gate. They were mean sods, the men in that family. I wonder sometimes how my mum put up with them, though I suppose with my dad being ill, and needing to be near a hospital, it was good of Uncle Joe to take us into the pub.

Uncle Joe was a betting man too, but making rather than taking bets. Often as not he'd have me running round to Ted Mead's with his fancy for the free-firty at Firff. Or he'd bang the counter with his big ham of a fist and bawl 'Steak!' 'Steak' was Ted's runner: biker to be more exact. He had this old black butcher's bike, complete with the basket on the front, which he'd lean against the side of the pub, and if you can say that a man looks like his dog, then 'Steak' looked like his bike. Tall and cadaverously thin, with glasses and a black cap so large that when he turned his head it stayed in the same place, he resembled a big black crow as he pedalled down the street, his elbows stuck out and his shoulders going up and down in time with his legs like wings. When you spoke to him he just nodded: never uttered a word. If he hadn't been a bookie's runner he'd probably have been a mortician.

I don't know why he was called 'Steak'. Maybe it was because we used to eat a lot of whale steaks just after the war. I don't think it could've been 'Stake', as in a bet or wager, because stake wasn't a word we used round our way in that context. It puzzled them at the hospital, too, when Uncle Joe was in there late in life. I'd just come out from visiting him, and I asked the sister how he was. All right, she said. But he kept sitting up in bed and yelling for steak. At first they thought he must've been hungry. But when they gave him steak he wouldn't eat it. Poor old bugger. I almost felt sorry for him.

Like Uncle Joe, the Sultan's gone now as well. There's still a pub there, but they've changed the name and tarted it up. There's a fruit machine in the corner where old Perce used to sit like a little gnome with his handkerchief knotted round his neck, his waistcoat full of watches, and his thick-lens glasses like the bottoms of Guinness bottles. But then as I've said, the whole community has gone now – except for those in the cemetery and they're not going anywhere.

The cemetery's still at the end of the road, but I don't know about the parade of shops across from it where, by a master-stroke of planning, the barber shop was right next door to the pie shop and every kid went into the barber's with his head full of stories about Sweeney Todd and the men came out with pieces of fag paper stuck to their faces where he'd cut them shaving. As kids we'd sit in the chair looking at the contraceptive signs and wonder what it was all about: and as the older men got out of the chair and felt in their pocket for some change, the barber would look at the display card, then at the customer, and ask with just the hint of a smile, 'Something for the weekend, sir?'

4 Up the hammers

Some people you meet in life you never forget. Casey was like that: a right tearaway, always in trouble. Which wasn't surprising considering his old man was a proper villain. When it came to breaking the law, Casey was a chip off the old block. It was common knowledge with me and my mates that if you wanted to be led astray, all you had to do was get mixed up with Casey.

I got involved with him because I passed my eleven-plus (the best reason they ever had for doing away with it). Don't ask me how I managed to pass. I hated school from the moment I was old enough to go. My mum said the reason I grew to six feet tall was that I was stretched at an early age from me clinging to Georgie Dance's lamp post and her pulling me by my feet in the direction of school. But pass the eleven-plus I did, and that meant I was sent to Plaistow Grammar School. Mum was very proud and pleased – until she found out that she'd have to fork out for a uniform and all the things that went with going to a school like that. Plaistow Grammar, you see, was one of those educational institutions that did its best to elevate the traditions of the grammar school, though its image wasn't helped by the biology mistress, who roared into the schoolyard every morning on a mud-splattered scrambler motorbike.

The headmaster was more the thing. He wore a cap and gown and used to swan around the corridors swishing his cane and tapping everything that moved. I think he saw himself as a latter-day Mr Chips, put on this earth to bring discipline and learning to the underprivileged kids in the East End. The trouble was, the last thing the underprivileged kids in the East End wanted was discipline and learning, and most of

Aged eleven, wearing the Plaistow Grammar School uniform.

them knew exactly how to avoid it. I was no exception: nor was Casey.

We were in the same class in my first year there, and it wasn't long before we became partners in crime. At the time of the story I'm about to tell I was trying to get some money together to buy a fishing rod that one of the other kids' fathers was selling: and in Casey's book that made me a good candidate for being an accomplice.

'Oi, Brownie!' he said one day, sidling up to me, all confidential like, his head flicking from side to side like a Wimbledon umpire's. You'd think, seeing him, that his head was on a permanent swivel – or that he was always on the lookout for the Old Bill. Casey never looked you in the eye when he talked to you, which wasn't surprising the speed at which his head was moving. He seemed to think the shifty approach was right: a bit of guilty conscience and a bit of wanting to tell you something really important but dead private. That way you were supposed to get the feeling you were dealing with a regular villain.

'Oi, Brownie!' Flick, flick. 'Wanna make a few bob?'

'Lead me astray,' I said, thinking of the fishing rod.

'Nuts,' he said.

That's a bit mild coming from him, I thought.

'F-----g peanuts!'

That was more like the Casey I knew and mistrusted.

'There's a fortune in 'em.'

'Tell me more,' I said, wondering if it wasn't so much that his head was going as he was going off his head.

'What we do,' he said, 'is we go down to Percy Larkins', see, buy 'alf an 'undredweight of peanuts, stick 'em in bags and flog 'em outside Hupton Park for a tanner a bag. I've worked it all out, Brownie; we can make quids at it.'

'Why me?' I asked, because I knew Casey didn't do anyone favours where money was concerned. 'Why don't you do it on your own?'

'I tried that,' he said. 'A couple of weeks ago. Trouble is I can't go back to Percy Larkins' for more nuts, can I?'

'I don't know. You tell me.'

'Well,' he leant forward confidentially. 'It's like this, see. I was just feelin' the weight of the bag, seein' whether or not I could carry it 'ome on me own, when they caught up wiv me. 'Course I paid up straight-away, but I don't think they'll let me 'ave any more. So it's down to you to buy the nuts. We'll split fifty-fifty, OK?'

OK by me it was, and as that weekend West Ham were playing at home, Saturday afternoon found us outside Upton Park. As well as half the school, all with home-made trays trying to flog bags of Percy Larkins' peanuts. Still, we sorted ourselves out a pitch, set up shop and were soon doing a roaring trade. It wasn't good enough for Casey, though. He wasn't satisfied.

'There's too much competition,' he said. 'You 'ang on 'ere, Brownie, 'n' I'll see what I can do.'

So saying he disappeared into the crowd in the direction of the nearest peanut salesman, a kid from the same class as us. I don't know what he said to him – Casey's lips never moved enough for lip-reading – but a few minutes later he came back munching peanuts and the kid had gone. This happened four or five times, and for all that Casey wasn't doing too much actual selling, his little absences were really good for business. In three-quarters of an hour we'd sold most of our nuts and were thinking of packing up when I spotted a blue dome bob-bob-bobbing above the crowd, heading in our direction. I turned to Casey, only he wasn't there. And like the Red Sea in that film in which Ben Hur plays Moses, the crowd parted and there stood the Old Bill – plus a couple of kids with trays piled high with unsold bags of peanuts. One kid had his old man with him.

'Where's that little bleeder Casey?' asked the dad.

'Who?' I answered. 'Never 'eard of 'im.'

The kid did his nut.

'Don't you tell lies, you.' He started to cry. 'You was wiv 'im, you was, you. I saw you. You 'n' 'im was wiv wunanuvver, you was.'

Good old Plaistow Grammar, I thought. Then, in his frustration, the kid lunged at me with his peanut tray. The copper stepped in to pull us apart, knocking over the other kid as he did so, and before you could blink peanuts were bouncing everywhere. The first kid's dad made a grab for me, but the copper got in the way and his helmet went flying. The large crowd gathering let out a cheer at this and I ducked down on to the pavement, shut my eyes and prayed. All I could hear was shouting from above and a loud crunching from ground level as the copper stumbled about on the peanuts, trying to find his helmet. I opened my eyes and caught a quick glimpse of Casey, grinning at me through the legs. Then I was being hauled to my feet.

'Right!' said the law. 'What's going on here – then?' he added, remembering his training.

I tried to explain.

'We was just trying to earn a bit of extra pocket money as my mum needed an operation done by a Swiss surgeon and we couldn't afford to buy any food and what's more me dad's so poor he can't afford to buy me a cap so's I can look out of the window and . . .'

The copper cut me short.

'Look,' he said, 'it's bad enough you kids breaking the law selling things in public in the first place without this other little bleeder – what's 'is name, Casey? – trying to come the strong-arm stuff. So piss off, the lot of you, before I run you all in.'

I didn't need telling twice. I made a quick exit, leaving the kid's dad arguing with the copper – a futile pastime. At the bus stop, who should I see but my old business partner, Casey, holding a big brown paper bag.

'What 'appened to you?' he asked, then cut me short as soon as I began to explain. 'Never mind now,' he said. ''Ere's the bus. Let's go round to my place and count the takings.'

So we went round to Casey's house and in the back way, down the little alley that ran beside the house. Through the kitchen window I could see his mum cutting up sandwiches for tea.

''Ello boys,' she said as we came in. 'How did you get on?'

'We did all right,' I said, emptying my pockets on to the table and counting the spoils. 'Two and a half quid profit, I reckon.'

'You're not saying much for yourself, Tommy,' said Casey's mother. While counting the money I'd noticed him shuffling about the room, trying to hide something, and now his mum had noticed it too.

'What've you got there?'

Not waiting for his reply, she made a quick grab behind him and came up with the brown paper bag which she straightaway up-ended on the kitchen table. Out rolled the copper's helmet. Not only that, the cheeky bugger had filled it full of peanuts!

'You wait till your dad gets home,' she said. ''E won't 'alf give you a thrashing.'

But Casey never did get his thrashing. Because while we were having our tea, his old man came down the side alley, spotted the copper's helmet on the kitchen table and did a bunk. Nobody saw him again for six weeks.

What with my association with Casey and my attendance record – non-attendance record was more like it – it didn't take old Mr Chips with his swishing cane more than a year to tumble to the fact that I wasn't doing much to elevate Plaistow Grammar; and that Plaistow Grammar was wasting its time trying to elevate me. We parted amicably enough, Plaistow Grammar and me, but I wasn't sorry to be leaving. For one thing Dennis and my mates from Hilda Road primary were at my new school, Pretoria Road (around there it was all Boer War names: Kimberley Road, Mafeking Road, Ladysmith Road – I never felt so relieved in all my life); for another it was closer to home so I got a few more minutes' kip in the mornings. But most important of all, I could leave school at fifteen and get on with the business of earning a living. Whereas if I'd remained at Plaistow Grammar, I'd have had to stay till I was sixteen, by which time I'd have been a well-educated villain.

As schools go, Pretoria Road was a good one: at least I was happy there and I got on well with most of the teachers. Mind you, some of the teachers got on pretty well with each other too. A new French mistress arrived one term, complete with the biggest pair of knockers I'd ever seen. And to show them off she used to wear these tight, bright red jumpers. There were kids wanting to do French that term who didn't know where Fenchurch Street was, let alone France. (This was before West Ham were playing in Europe and places like Borussia Mönchengladbach, Dynamo Dresden and Haladas Szombathely had become as familiar to your average East End kid as the Barking Road.)

One morning I came out of class into the playground at break to find most of the school lined up along a classroom window. In those days all the classrooms had these blacked-out windows, except for a foot or so of plain glass at the top to let you know it was still daylight outside. I suppose the idea was to stop the kids gazing out of the windows when they were bored with the lessons – which except for French was most of the time. That day all the kids were doing their best to look *into* the classroom: standing on each other's shoulders to see through the glass at the top.

'What's going on?' I asked: but as no one answered me the only way to find out was to have a dekko for myself. I persuaded a couple of kids to leave their vantage point and clambered on to the vacant shoulders to peer inside. There was the French teacher and one of the men teachers: very close together, him with his hands up inside her jumper, and jig-a-jigging along a row of desks like a pair of prancing ponies. Just then he came up for air – and his eyes caught that long row of eyes looking through the window at them. His hands came out of her jumper, they both rushed out of the classroom and that was the last we saw of them. The teachers as well. By the time we went back into class after the break they had gone from the school. Just like that.

For the life of me I can't remember who the other teacher was or what he taught. It wasn't Mr Smith though, I know that. If he'd gone there'd have been great rejoicing, for if there was one teacher at Pretoria Road who believed in discipline, it was Smiffy. He was the PT master, wouldn't you know. Fit as a fiddle; never wore socks; looked like an ex-petty officer; fond of the cane and Fonda of the exercise yard. He whistled the same tuneless song through his teeth in time to all those awful physical jerks he'd have us doing: sort of aerobics for young anarchists. We had to take it seriously too or we'd be pretty quickly whacked. One afternoon a gang of sixth form girls were taking the mickey out of us through the barbed wire and Smiffy got mad. He grabbed the ringleader, dragged her into our compound, bent her over and caned her in front of us all. If he'd done it today it would have been headlines in *The Sun*: 'Physical Jerker Spanks Sexy Schoolgirl'. Instead they made him deputy headmaster.

The boys shared the same building as the girls, but it was split down the middle, just as the yard was separated by a high wire fence. The girls went through one gate, the boys through another. And we were searched each morning as we went into school. For matches more than anything else, most of us being budding arsonists as far as school buildings were concerned. But being searched did mean we couldn't carry cigarettes, which didn't sadden Cyril at the corner shop. Instead he did a roaring trade in his special line: cigarettes for twopence each, plus an extra halfpenny to light it for you. 'Tuppenny fag 'n' a ha'penny light, Cyril' was the cry as soon as school was out. Then off we'd go, puffing away to our heart's content.

Still, you're only young once, unless you never grow up, and no one ever told us that smoking was like the national health – it damaged your health. All they told us was that it stunted your growth, and when there were kids around like Fatty Risby, who grew in all directions, there wasn't much evidence of stunting to be seen. Poor old Risby. He had a hard time of it at school, always being bullied because he was fat. Not surprising really that he developed a grudge against the world, but that was no reason for going off to join the police cadets. I mean, around our way that does make you the black sheep of the family. Even worse, what's the first thing he does when he gets his helmet? He nicks his old man for receiving!

Years later, when I had a hit record riding high in the charts, I went back to pay Pretoria Road a visit. Showing off a bit, I guess, but also to let them know I hadn't forgotten them now I was famous. I was driving a white Austin Healey 3000 at the time, and in the true style of the American pop stars we were all imitating, I dressed myself up in a matching white suit. And to make sure I *really* made an impact, I waited round the corner till it was playtime before roaring through the gates and screeching to a halt in the middle of the playground. Hordes of admiring kids immediately swarmed around the car. But I hadn't been educated at Pretoria Road Secondary Modern for nothing. I knew the form. Sorting out the biggest and toughest looking kid, I slipped him a fiver, saying 'Look after the motor, son.' (Always a wise move.) Then, signing autographs as I went, I made my way to the head's study.

Mr Roberts, the headmaster, greeted me like a long-lost son and insisted on taking me round to see all my old teachers during the afternoon lessons. Every classroom we visited was an ego boost. The teachers seemed pleased to see me and the kids were all agog. Till finally we came to Mr Wilson's class. Joe Wilson was the music teacher, and as I'd been top of the class in music and was now making a living from it, I felt very proud going back to see him. In we went and there, at the piano as always, sat Mr Wilson. 'Look who I've got here now,' announced Mr Roberts in his sing-song Welsh accent.

The room went quiet. Old Joe Wilson stood up and came towards me, his head moving frontways, his body sidling sideways. He was shaking with emotion: I was really touched. About three feet away (two of mine and his front one) he began to lift his arm and I raised mine to shake his hand. Only his kept travelling upwards until a quivering finger was pointing right between my eyes.

'Out!' he screamed. 'Get out!'

I looked behind me. Nobody there. He must mean me, I thought.

'Get out!' he screamed again, his voice bordering on hysteria.

I was stunned. Where was the hero's welcome?

'Yes, you, Brown. Out! You're debauching the arts!'

It suddenly occurred to me that after years of trying to teach us 'The Ash Grove' and 'Who is Sylvia?', poor old Joe was hardly likely to get up from his piano and say 'Rock 'n' roll's not my bag, man.'

Poor old Joe. I never did see him again. Or Mr Roberts. Or Smiffy. They say that the more famous you become, the more you don't want to know your old mates. But I've found the contrary to be more the truth. It seemed to me that my old mates no longer wanted to know me. It was almost as if they assumed that I didn't want to know them, and they never gave me a chance to prove otherwise. Even worse, they never gave me credit for not changing simply because I'd made a few quid for myself.

I did see Casey again though – and he was trying to sell me something. After leaving Plaistow Grammar I soon lost touch with him – probably a good thing – so it came as some surprise when, years later when I was in the West End in *Charlie Girl*, I answered the front door and who should be standing there, looking over both shoulders at once, but Casey.

''Ello, Brownie,' he said, his eyes sizing up the mansion I was living in at the time and taking in the Healey and the E-Type in the drive. 'I 'eard you done well for y'self.'

I invited him in, wondering if I could introduce him to Vicki, my wife, as a peanut-selling partner from way back.

'No, no, can't stay, Brownie. In a rush,' he said, all confidential like, so I'd get the impression that the Old Bill was just one step behind him. 'I been doin' all right for myself too, y' know, son. What d'ya think?' he asked, showing me several pounds of solid gold wrapped round the workings of a wrist watch. 'Nice, eh. Good whistle, eh?' And it was, if you like that sort of East End spiv-on-the-make look in fashion. 'Like the motor, Brownie?' he asked, pointing to the Mark 10 Jag standing in the drive behind him.

'Very smart, Tommy,' I told him, beginning to wonder what his game was and what all this was about. Bit of protection, maybe: that would've been in Casey's line. 'Sure you won't come in for a bit?'

'No, no, Brownie, must rush.' His head went on the swivel again. 'Got something I thought might interest you. In the motor,' he added conspiratorially.

Bloody hell, I thought, he's a fence. But what's he trying to pass off? The way his old head was going I couldn't tell whether he was nervous,

The Brown family at home – my wife Vicki and children Samantha and Pete!

suspicious or just his old sweet Casey self. We walked down to the car and Casey opened the boot.

'You'll like these, Brownie,' he said, pulling a suitcase forward. 'Bit of class.' My mind was working overtime now. It had to be jewellery or watches, I reckoned, half expecting the law to come tearing up the drive any minute. Casey opened the suitcase.

'There y'are, Brownie. What d'ya think?'

I looked into the suitcase. It was full of ties!

5 I've been working on the railroad

Given my early career – totting copper wire, running the power supply to the neighbourhood eel stall – it was only natural my first full-time job should be as an electrician's apprentice. This was a natural progression, except that I didn't make much progress. The firm of electricians was called Grimmer and Company, and the job lived up to their name. I was nothing but a glorified tea-boy and sweeper-upper, and the sort of money they paid me – two pounds ten a week plus my fares – I could've made in a few hours selling peanuts outside West Ham Football Club.

Mind you, my next job was even worse. It was in the packing department of a printers in Covent Garden, and if nothing else it didn't half put me off unions. My first job every day, I was told, was to go around all the offices with an insecticide spray: though why anyone should want to bug the place was beyond me. The first two days someone came round with me to show me the way and make sure I didn't drown in the typing pool; the third day I was on my own, which was all right because to tell you the truth I didn't find spraying offices too much of a drain on my brain. I flitted round the building in no time at all, and that was just where I got it wrong. No sooner had I stepped back into the packing department, ready for my next job, than these two heavies grabbed me and stuck me in a cupboard.

'That job,' they said, 'takes an hour and a half, and you've done it in three-quarters of an hour.'

Bang went the cupboard door and that was that. I had to stay there until the hour and a half was up. Then I could start my next job. If I'd known it was going to be like this, I thought, I could've brought my guitar and practised a few licks of 'Don't you rock me, daddy'o' or 'The Rock Island Line'. But they'd probably have put their foot down on that as well, and I couldn't afford a new guitar with the sort of money they were paying me. Sometimes I was hard pushed to buy a packet of fags: hard pushed to smoke them too on one occasion. I got stuck in the service lift with Charlie, one of the old packers, and very frightening it was too, because the lift kept dropping then stopping and dropping then stopping and we couldn't even have a smoke to calm our nerves. We each had a packet of fags but we didn't have a match between us, except for the one that old Charlie used for picking his teeth and that was dead.

My next job, though, I really enjoyed – working on the railway. For a start it was just a step and a jump through the cemetery at the bottom of our road to the depot (a pretty quick step and a jump if you were on night shift). And being on shifts meant I had more time for playing with the skiffle group I was in. In fact, it was through the drummer in the group, Sid Rothwell, that I'd heard there was a job going. Sid had been with Eastern Region ever since he left school, but around this time he was feeling like a change. His big problem was that he didn't know what to do, so as he'd helped me find a job, I went round looking with him to help him out. Eventually I saw there was a vacancy at a furniture factory nearby, and as he had a good track record on the railway they took him on: said he could start the following week. But the very first day there he cut off three fingers on a circular saw – didn't know they were gone until he came to say goodnight to the foreman! His wife, unfairly I thought, always blamed me for what happened, though I tried to reassure her by pointing out it could have been worse. I don't think she got it, so maybe it was worse than I was told at the time.

I began my time on the railway as a cleaner in the days of steam engines, and by the time I left I'd become a fireman. The knack of cleaning, I soon discovered, was not so much the way you moved your elbow as the way the engine came in and went out of the depot. If you got its schedule right, all you had to do was clean the front, back and one of the sides because that was all the foreman could see from his little shed as the engine went out. Mind you, he could've come out and walked right round the engine and tender, but that would have been too much like hard work. He hadn't been promoted to foreman to spend all day walking around the cleaning pit inspecting engines. And of course he couldn't jump over the pit to have a quick look. Jumping over the pits was the first thing you were told *not* to do when you joined the railway. So one side of the engine went out dirty, and next day some

Working on the railway!

poor sod would probably get an engine with two days' grime on one side. But then he'd also leave one side and so it went on. The railway was full of 'wrinkles' like that.

The firelighters, for example, got away with murder, though in some cases they were lucky to get away without being murdered. It was their job to start the fires and have the engines nicely warmed up for when the drivers and firemen came on duty; but at our depot they seemed to spend most of their time sitting in the smokebox of an engine playing cards. They'd leave open the door at the front of the engine to get some air and light, but to all intents and purposes you wouldn't know they were there; except that if you couldn't find them you'd know pretty well that's exactly where they'd be.

I reported for duty one night on a midnight shift for a turn that was known as 'the golden mile', so called because you could sit in your engine all night in the shunting yards on double time waiting for a job. Some nights there'd be nothing to do at all. This night there was. I'd been assigned to take a load of goods wagons down to Tilbury.

'Who'm I with?' I asked the foreman.

'Passed Fireman Menzies,' he replied.

'Oh no!' I blurted out. 'Not Mad Menzies.'

'Right first time!' growled a voice right behind me. It was him, Mad Menzies. 'Grab your gear, Brownie. Engine 80079. She should be steaming by now.'

Out we shuffled from the foreman's office, across the freezing cold shed towards our appointed engine.

'Hey, Menzies,' I said as we got closer, 'if that's our engine, she looks bloody cold.'

'You're right,' said Menzies. 'Who's on the firelighting shift then?'

I kept quiet.

'I bet it's that bloody Ashami,' snarled Menzies. 'The lazy bastard! If I have to sit on my arse all night again, waiting for a hot engine, I'll have his guts for garters.'

'I'll go and find him,' I said, imagining Ashami's intestines laced around Mrs Menzies' nether regions.

'No you won't,' said Menzies. 'We'll both go. And I hope for his sake that you find him first.'

Ashami was legendary around Plaistow loco yard for his ingenuity in finding places to kip while he was supposed to be on duty. Once, in a rare burst of railway efficiency, some energetic foreman had organized a military-style search for our elusive dusky pimpernel. There were sixteen of us in all: cleaners, passed cleaners, firemen and two old drivers who knew every skive in the book. We spread out across the engine shed and, working to a grid system, meticulously searched every inch of the yard: wagons, guards' vans, engines, even the coal tenders on the big old WDs (War Department engines). Three of us were set to raking over the coal itself with shovels.

'Don't be too careful,' we were told. 'If you cut his bloody head off, it serves him right.'

But he wasn't to be found.

It turned out that he was sleeping where no one ever dreamt of looking, though when you think about it, it was the logical place for Ashami to be – kipping in the firelighters' rest room.

This particular night, however, it looked as if Menzies and I had a mammoth task ahead of us. After all, the aforementioned search had been conducted in broad daylight. Menzies and I were looking for him at a quarter to one in the morning and Ashami was as black as Newgate's knocker. He only had to close his eyes and the Berkeley Hunt couldn't find him. I ventured to suggest the unwritten sin of the footplate staff.

'Let's report him to the foreman. It's about time someone did.'

Menzies' jaw dropped. He gasped as if someone had hit him in the stomach. I waited in silence, fearing what he was going to say. The words began to rattle in the back of his throat.

'Bloody good idea, Brownie,' he said. 'But first of all get up on that footplate and make sure the fire wasn't started then went out on its own. There's no point in getting him the sack unless we have to. After all,' added Menzies with a magnanimity I didn't know he had in him, 'everyone's got his good points, even Ashami.'

'Such as?' I asked, not being able to think of any.

'He's a rotten poker player,' said Menzies. 'I've taken his wages off him for the past three weeks and my old lady's beginning to get used to the good life. There's no point in kicking a gift horse in the mouth.'

I clambered up on the footplate and looked in through the firebox door. Not a glimmer of light. But just as I was about to shout down to Menzies, I heard a rasping sound – a cough? – followed by a loud, contented sigh. It had come from the firebox itself. I rummaged in my bag for my bike torch and, very cautiously, shone it through the hole. There was Ashami, curled up like a six-foot baby, sound asleep among the coal and the oily cotton waste which he'd put there to light the fire. Quietly I climbed down from the cab and reported to Menzies.

'The bugger's asleep in the firebox,' I told him. 'The fire's all set. It's just that he hasn't lit it.'

Menzies thought for a moment, and for a horrible second it looked as if he was going to smile.

'Poor bastard,' he said. 'I bet he's had a hard day. Maybe we should help him out a bit, eh Brownie? You nip over to the bench and get me a big lump of oily waste. We'll light the fire for him.'

I did as I was bid. When I got back to the engine Menzies was on the footplate waiting. I threw up the waste and climbed up to join him.

'Where's Ashami?' I asked.

'Oh, he's gone,' replied Menzies. 'Or he bloody soon will be.' And so saying he threw the lighted cotton into the firebox.

I don't think even Menzies was prepared for what happened next. There was a low, ominous 'whoof' followed closely by a piercing scream. Then Ashami shot out through the firebox door – an aperture no more than eighteen inches high – without even touching the sides. He was as white as a sheet and shaking like a blancmange. Not even pausing to thank Menzies for lighting the fire for him he leapt straight from the cab to the ground and was off across the shed like a scalded cat, jumping over the pits as he went.

With the Game for a Laugh *team – Henry Kelly, Matthew Kelly and Sarah Kennedy.*

'Fancy a game of poker?' shouted Menzies after the retreating Ashami.

'You're mad, Menzies,' I said between my laughter. 'Bloody mad.'

As a postscript to this story, some twenty-odd years later a research assistant at London Weekend Television was trying to establish Menzies' whereabouts because they wanted to surprise me on a show called *Game for a Laugh.* When she phoned British Rail's personnel office and asked if they knew of a driver called David Menzies who used to work at Plaistow yards, the bloke on the phone said without hesitation, 'Oh, you mean Mad Menzies. Yes, he's a driver down at Ripple Lane.'

The great thing about the railway, as far as I was concerned, was the amount of unpaid leave they let me have, especially as by my second year working there I was getting more and more gigs with the band I was in, the Spacemen Skiffle Group. I'd started in a skiffle group at a youth club while I was still at school: the Ace of Clubs Rhythm Group. We had a great argument about how we should spell rhythm and in the end I got my way, which is why the cards we had printed said the Ace of Clubs Rythim Group. I was good at getting what I wanted. Later, in the Spacemen, I decided we needed a proper bass rather than the standard tea-chest job, so while Pete Oakman was at work one day I took his guitar down to the local music centre and traded it in for a bass. When Pete came home he discovered he had a new role in life.

I'd met Pete and his brother Tony while playing with the Ace of Clubs and they'd asked me to join their group. It was probably the first break I'd had, especially as it brought me into contact with their parents. Albert and Frances Oakman had a small newsagent and tobacconist's shop in Leyton, and it was there that I found the only real encouragement I'd had as far as music was concerned. They were like a mum and dad to me. Mrs O. was a wonderful pianist, while Albert wasn't too bad except that he could only play one tune: it was called 'You're the Cream in my Coffee' – and he could only play *that* on the black notes. What was so great about Mrs O. was her patience. Being of Italian descent she knew lots of Italian folk songs, which she'd play

Mrs Oakman demonstrating her skills on the piano.

My first group, the Ace of Clubs Rhythm Group, in 1957–8 (I'm on the extreme left). Note the standard tea-chest bass!

on the piano for hours while I learnt them on the guitar. She was a real inspiration.

Thinking back now, I realize what great, happy times those were. There were about eight of us in the band, and every spare moment we used to cram ourselves into the small storeroom at the back of the shop with our guitars, tea-chest bass and the inevitable washboard. I don't know how Mr and Mrs Oakman put up with us. Don't know how they could *afford* to put up with us, come to that. I had this passion for ice-cream cones and was always asking Albert if he had any broken ones. When the answer was no I used to nudge one of the cardboard boxes in the storeroom with my elbow, so ensuring a regular supply. It took me years after that to play the guitar without my arm going in and out like the piston on a steam engine.

Poor old Albert. What with the skiffle group keeping him up all night and having to start work at five-thirty every morning with the newspapers, plus the fact that we used to con him into taking us to gigs in his Ford Prefect, he had a bit of a hard time. Add to that all the trips he had to make to the factory for ice-cream cones and wafers and it wasn't surprising that he didn't have time to learn more than one tune.

The Spacemen Skiffle Group started off good and got better all the time. Playing around the local pubs and clubs and appearing in talent

The Spacemen Skiffle Group. We had a proper bass by now.

shows we were earning quite a name for the group even if we weren't earning much money. But nobody cared about money as long as we were enjoying ourselves. Then skiffle turned to rock and roll and it wasn't long before I was spending more time on the stage than I was on the footplate of an engine. I wasn't aware of it happening, but the music simply caught up with me, and before I knew it I was a professional musician. I'd fired my last engine.

6 Bald at Butlins

I was doing a gig with the Spacemen in a pub called the Lion and Key in Leyton when Bill, the landlord, came up during a break to say some geezer was trying to get hold of me. He'd left a number to call, which I did as soon as I'd tasted one of the pints Bill had brought us.

'Hello, mate. Joe Brown.'

'Good of you to call, my son. A mate of mine's got a problem. Wonders if you might like to help him out. He's got a season lined up at Butlins but his lead guitarist's let him down. Thought you might be interested.'

'Yeah, might be. Where's it at?'

'Somewhere up in Yorkshire. Place called Filey.'

'Never 'eard of it, mate. Sounds like it's all black pudding and crumpet in curlers.'

'That's Lancashire, you daft twat.'

'All the same to me, mate. Norf of Epping Forest.'

'Well, do you want to do it or not?'

'Yeah, I'll do it. What's the band?'

'Clay Nicholls and the Blue Flames.'

And they were awful. The worst group I've ever played in. In fact we were so bad that the audience used to get up on the stage and fight with us rather than have to listen to us. Even the camp commandant thought we were terrible.

'Look, you lot,' he told us after the first week, 'either you get your act together, get a gimmick, or get out.'

When he'd gone we told him what he could get. But we had to admit he did have a point. If we weren't going to get any better – and that needed a miracle – then what we needed was a gimmick. The question

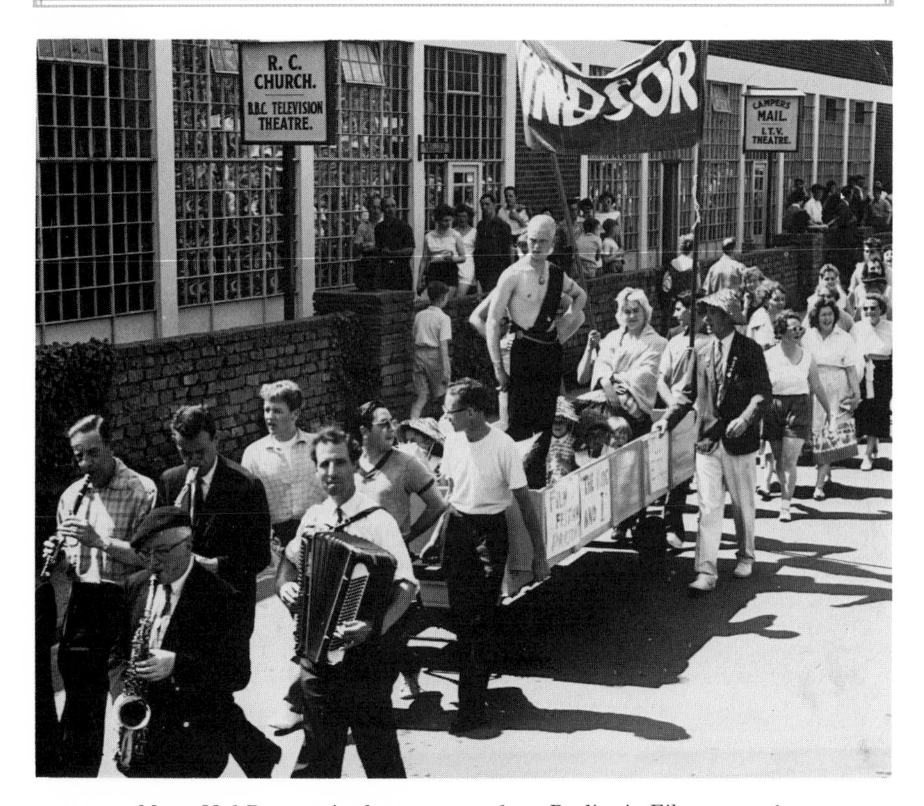

Me as Yul Brynner in the camp parade at Butlins in Filey, 1959–60.

was what. As usual it was Joe Brown who had the brainwave.

'I know,' I announced, 'I'll shave me 'ead.'

They looked at me as if I'd just played G with my fingers on the right strings.

'I'll use that razor they've got on display down at the chemists',' I explained. 'We'll pass the word round; get all the kids down there. It'll be good publicity for the shop as well as us.'

Next morning after roll-call we all rolled up to the chemists' shop. The place was packed.

'Must've been a busy night last night,' said the Drummer.

First of all I had to cut off most of my hair, then I got to work on what was left with the razor. After that, just so nobody could mistake me for Yul Brynner, the boys painted a red, white and blue target on top of my head. We repeated this performance every morning, and as a gimmick it was a great success. Plenty of people came along each day to see the idiot from the band shave his head, and we attracted good

My trademark – blond spiky hair.

crowds to the ballroom at night. The fights continued, of course, because although our gimmick was good our music remained terrible.

Worse than that, though, was that I couldn't get away with anything with the girls – and being Butlins there were plenty of them about. Everyone in the camp knew who 'the bald-headed git with the painted nob' was. Fair ruined my chances, that did, especially as being in the band was supposed to improve your chances with the girls. Oh well, the things you do for fame.

One good thing did come out of shaving my head, though. It gave me an image. Before I got to work with the razor, my hair had been straight and lank: I had to use a jar of grease on it every time I wanted a quiff – and a quiff was essential in those early days of rock and roll. However, when my hair grew again it grew straight up and I kept it that way. Blond spiky hair was my trademark and that's how people remember me even now.

A week went by and we had another visit from the camp commandant.

'All right, you lot. You're still not worth your salt as a band, so unless you want to be off-loaded you're going to have to pull your weight around the camp. What about it then? Can any of you do anything else except that rubbish you call music?'

Playing at the Deep Litter Club in Lichfield. The horse brasses on my guitar strap came in useful if fans turned hostile.

'Such as?' we asked.

'Well,' he thought for a moment. 'Can anyone ride?'

'My grandfather was a trick rider with Buffalo Bill's Wild West Show,' I said. Which is true; he was.

'Right then,' said the commandant. 'You'll help the riding instructor.'

Me, I'd never been on a horse in my life, but I managed somehow. And the girls never much minded about the instruction as long as they had something between their legs that moved. Cleaning out the stables one day, though, I found a load of old horse brasses which I thought would be just the thing to attach to my guitar strap. They came in useful when the crowd attacked the stage that night.

'Better wi' guitar strap than th'art wi' guitar,' said one punter in admiration as I laid him low with several pounds of flying horse brass.

The sad thing is that the camp commandant agreed with him, and it was not long before I was back in London playing with the Oakmans. And that was when I first heard from Larry Parnes.

7 The Parnes

Larry Parnes had a talent for two things: making money and making up names. Johnny Gentle, Dickie Pride, Duffy Power, Vince Eager, Marty Wilde – all were singers on Larry's books in the rock 'n' rollin' fifties and sixties, and he must've had more names where they came from because he was always holding auditions to find more singers for his stable of pop stars. Talk about flogging a dead horse. It was through one of these auditions that I came into contact with him. Not because I wanted to be a singer but because Larry wanted a guitarist for auditions he was holding in Southend for Jack Good's new TV show, *Boy Meets Girls*, which was to be the follow-up in 1959 to his *Oh Boy!* show.

'Ten shillings for the night,' said Larry when I went to see him at his office. 'And you get to play in the Beat Boys for the show as well.' That was the Parnes all over. Signs you up for a small gig like an audition for ten bob and you find you're also playing in his band for two houses. Besides which there was no mention of expenses.

'You ever run a jellied eel stall?' I asked him, having reckoned that it would cost me a couple of quid for the night's work. Still, if stars like Vince Eager were on the bill, I reckoned I'd made the big time. Some things in life, I told myself, you just have to pay for. That was Larry's philosophy as well, so long as he wasn't the one who had to do the paying.

Playing at Southend was a bit like playing a home fixture, the number of times I'd been there on pub outings, and even if I hadn't known where the Odeon was, I'd have soon found it by following the screaming fans and policemen with dogs. It'd be worth paying ten bob for this, I thought, forgetting that I'd already paid to get there and would probably have to buy my own nosh. I showed my guitar to the doorman.

'Hofner,' he said, which I took to be Hungarian for 'That's all right, mate, in you go' and waltzed past him. They got a lot of refugees in Southend after the war.

Upstairs on stage it was pandemonium. Most of Larry's big names were there, airing their egos and trying to work out their acts. As I recall, we even had the makings of a fist-fight over who was going to sing 'Hound Dog', at which stage Vince Eager said, 'Sod this for a lark. I'm going to get some fish and chips.'

Off he went and gradually we finished the run-through. At six o'clock up went the tabs for the first show and we were off. Considering we knew only three chords we did remarkably well and I thoroughly enjoyed myself – especially when Vince Eager came on. Six feet four of gold lamé suit, he sang in a high voice with a strong fast vibrato that put you in mind of someone sawing up aluminium. He said it was just his gimmick. Yes, the gimmick was all-important whether you were at Butlins or the Southend Odeon. You got on only if you did something different. My gimmick, I decided that night, would be to play a few licks from time to time.

It was doing something different that made Vince's act go down so well that evening. During rehearsals he'd noticed a large wooden apron which rose from the orchestra pit – probably used to raise and lower the long-since-gone organ – and he made up his mind that, towards the end of his act, he'd leap across the footlights and land on it. This would get him closer to the audience: he could really whip them into a frenzy at the climax of his act, and the punters would have a better look at the gold suit. After all, they'd paid for it.

The moment arrived.

'Yes, tonight, Josephine, yes toniii . . . ght . . .'

That was the song.

'Everything, Josephine, will be all rii . . . ght . . .'

Vince reached the last chorus and dramatic key change and, blinded by the footlights, leapt gracefully over the top of them on to the apron. Which, unknown to our gilded hero, had been lowered while he was away at the chip shop.

The coiled microphone cable shot out like Popeye's anchor chain. The band looked at one another.

There was a minim pause followed by a crotchet crash. It was a deep pit!

The front line of the Beat Boys stepped forward in time to the music and peered, cautiously, over the edge. Lying down there was what looked like a pile of gold.

'He's struck it rich,' said the Bass Player.

The pile moved and we heard a noise. Vince was still singing.

'Everything, Josephine, will be all right;

But not tonight, Josephine, not tonight.'

This must be what it's all about, I thought. (Yeah, man!)

When we did the second house, Vince came on, still in the gold lamé suit, with several hundredweight of plaster cast round his leg.

'To anchor him to the stage,' said the Bass Player, though in fact poor old Vince had broken his ankle. Rumour had it that Larry Parnes wouldn't let him cut off the trousers of the gold lamé suit so he had to wear them till the plaster came off. But at least he could tell people that he'd gone down well in Southend. Quickly too for that matter.

After the show came the auditions, and oh dear! It wasn't surprising that Jack Good wasn't buying singers that night. On the other hand someone did catch his attention.

'I don't want any of the singers,' he told Larry, 'but I'll have that lad on the guitar for the orchestra. Who's his manager?'

Here's me with my first contract, and other pieces of junk.

Up spake the Parnes in his best Damon Runyon.

'Why, it is nobody but me.'

And all of a sudden I had a manager.

'Come and see me at the office tomorrow,' Larry ordered afterwards. 'We'll finalize your contract.'

A manager and a contract, all in the same week – I was coming on fast. And if Larry had had his way I'd have had a new name as well.

'To start with,' he said the next day, 'you need a name. You can't walk around with a name like Joe Brown.'

'Why not?' I asked. 'Hundreds of other people do.'

'My point exactly,' he said, stabbing a finger at me. 'You need something that rolls off the tongue.'

Holy Harry, I thought. He wants to call me dribble.

He leant back in his chair, gazing at the ceiling and making pyramids with his fingers for about five minutes, waiting for inspiration to strike. I sat in nervous anticipation. My whole future depended on this moment. In twenty-five years' time I might be appearing in a television commercial with the name Darryl Dribble on my American Express card. Suddenly he shot forward in his chair and rested his hands on the desk, looking straight at me.

'Twitch,' he said.

I duly obliged.

'What's the matter with your face?' he asked in alarm.

'Nothing,' I said. 'I just twitched.'

'No, no, no, no, no. You don't understand. That's what we'll call you. Twitch. Elmer Twitch.'

I gaped at him.

'I think I prefer Dribble,' I said.

He ignored me.

'And of course you'll have a group. We'll call them The Fidgets. Elmer Twitch and The Fidgets. I can see it. I like it.'

I stood up to leave. He got the message.

'I suppose,' he said, looking downcast, 'we could always leave it as Joe Brown.'

The name settled, we got down to the less serious business as far as Larry was concerned. Money. He had that all worked out. I'd have a three-year contract, start at fifteen pounds a week, Larry would pay the instalments on my motorbike, and he'd move my mum, Pete and me out of the pub into a London flat that he'd pay for. It sounded great at the time. The only one of us that wasn't happy about it was the cat. It pined for its shrimps' heads.

Larry Parnes (left), Billy Fury (right) and Billy's road manager.

Larry's promise to take care of the HP payments on my bike was what really clinched the deal, of course. That bike was the pride of my life. Promoters must have wondered what they'd let themselves in for when they saw me turning up for gigs on a 650 BSA Road Rocket in black leathers with a guitar slung across my back. By the time I'd been with Larry for a year or so, though, I'd gone off motorbikes completely and had become the proud owner (HP again) of my first Austin Healey sports car. I kept the bike as well for a while, but as it was just gathering dust, in a moment of extreme benevolence I gave it to my cousin Jim. He rode it for some time (fair enough because I rode on his licence for long enough) until one day he came and asked if I'd mind him swapping it for a small sports car that a bloke in his street wanted to part with. Do what you like, I said. It's your bike. But three weeks after the swap Jim was on the phone.

'I don't half feel a fool,' he told me. 'That bloke I did the swap with just came round my house and told me that some HP company have repossessed the bike. They say no one's paid a penny on it in the last two and a half years.'

Good old Larry. Live now, pay never.

Our first flat was in Victoria. Billy Fury moved in with us and Mum thought looking after us was wonderful after years of being general dogsbody at the pub. But as the months went by I came to see exactly what I'd let myself in for. Being totally reliant on Larry for all my gigs and for our accommodation, I'd lost my independence. I first realized it when he moved us out of the Victoria flat into a place in Paddington which was little better than a dosshouse. He had his whole stable there at one time and Mum used to muck out every morning. I'm not joking. The place was so filthy that everybody got crabs, and even the cat thought they were a poor substitute for shrimps.

Before too long, Larry and I came to the conclusion that we didn't see eye to eye, which wasn't surprising given that the Parnes had eyes in the back of his head. I laugh about it now and admire him for his good business sense. In fact, I have a lot of respect for him, but there was a time when . . . I suppose when someone owns you, or you think they do, the only way to keep your self-respect is to rebel, and that's just what I did. We had some amazing ding-dongs and they were mostly my fault, not least because I could never resist sending him up. Larry, I need hardly add, did not have my sense of humour.

Vicki and me with my first Austin Healey sports car.

He took me to dinner at his parents' home one night, not because he wanted to (he made that pretty plain) but because his mother, for reasons best known to herself, had taken a shine to me. 'God knows why,' Larry said graciously as he briefed me on good behaviour and drilled me on table manners and social etiquette. I could see I was making him nervous.

Surprise number one came when a butler opened the door.

'Good evening, Mr Lawrence,' he said.

The Parnes shot me a look that said 'You dare show me up and . . .'; but it was too late. The cat was out of the bag. Mr Lawrence, eh! From then on it was Mr Lawrence this and Mr Lawrence that and good old Mr Lawrence, and there wasn't a thing Larry could do about it.

Mr and Mrs Parnes were wonderful people. They made me very welcome, and once I'd made a few trial runs at *their* sense of humour we got on fine. After the usual social chat about the weather, the season at Cannes, the stock market and how Mr Lawrence was ripping off all his artists, we settled down to the serious business of the evening: dinner. And such a dinner! The Parnes were Jewish, and the table was laid out as I'd never seen before with all kinds of fish. It was a truly beautiful sight. The others knew what to take, but for the first time since arriving I was at a loss. Larry's lectures on table manners hadn't mentioned fish.

Mrs Parnes, a lovely woman with a twinkle in her eye, put me out of my misery.

'What sort of fish would you like, Joey?' she asked.

'If it's all the same to you, Mrs Parnes,' I said, giving her a big wink that Larry couldn't see, 'I'd rather have a bacon sandwich.'

Larry almost choked to death.

'What's the matter, Lawrence?' asked his mother.

'Yes, Lawrence,' I echoed, 'what's the matter?'

But the Parnes had less to say than a Trappist monk with laryngitis. He just sat there gritting his teeth. It was a grand night.

8 Mum and the neighbours

After we'd been living for a month or so in the Paddington dosshouse, the RSPCA came along and said they'd take the cat into care unless we provided better accommodation for it. This was serious, so the Parnes rented a nice house for us in North Finchley. Very posh it was. The houses had doors that didn't open straight on to the street. 'That ain't natural,' my mum said. But you knew they'd heard all about Mum in North Finchley because everyone stood outside the pubs drinking their pints and their gins and tonics so she couldn't chuck them through the plate-glass windows.

The trouble was the neighbours. You'd think they'd have been over the moon at having a telly star living next door, but what with the late comings and goings of a hard-working rock 'n' roll singer, and Mum and me rowing most of the time, I think they could see the price of property in the area taking a nose-dive. And if there's one thing they get concerned about in North Finchley, it's anything to do with noses.

One morning, after a good old shout-up the night before, Mum put on her duffel coat and Marks & Sparks slippers, men's size eight, and shuffled off to the shops in search of some pork sausages. I knew she'd gone out because the door slamming woke me up from this dream I'd been having about Petula Clark. For a minute I thought it must have been true love because the whole house was shaking. Then the doorbell rang. My brother Pete answered the door while I lay in bed and listened. It was the Woman Next Door.

Pete: 'Yes?'

WND: 'Just what's going on these days in North Finchley?'

Pete: 'Sorry, Missus.'

WND: 'Don't you realize that *some people* have to work for a living?'
Pete: 'Sorry, Missus.'
WND: 'Any more of this rowdy behaviour and I'll send my husband round.'
Pete: 'Sorry, Missus.'
The door was closed so gently I hardly heard it.
Three days later the same thing happened. Late home, row with Mum, woken up by the door slamming, then the doorbell.
Pete: 'Yes?'
WND: 'Just what's going on these days in North Finchley?'
Pete: 'Sorry, Missus.'
WND: 'Don't you realize that some people have *to work* for a living?'
Pete: 'Sorry, Missus.'
WND: 'Any more of this rowdy behaviour and I'll send my husband round.'
Pete: 'Sorry, Missus.'
The door closed gently. I must admit that by this time I felt a bit sorry for Pete. On no account, I told him, let Mum know about it. She wouldn't be as polite as he was, and the last thing we wanted was a feud with the neighbours. For one thing I couldn't see the Parnes coughing up for windows as frequently as the brewery did. So a week went by, during which Mum and I settled into an uneasy truce. But like all good things truces don't last forever. I came home from a gig about three o'clock one morning, and when all I wanted to do was go to bed and dream, there was Mum in her size eight M & Ss, waiting for a ding-dong. I forget how the argument started, but then I always did.
Next morning, when the three of us were having breakfast, there came a ring on the doorbell.
'Oo the bleedin' 'ell's that at this hour of the mornin'?' asked Mum.
I looked at Pete, Pete looked at me, we both looked at Mum.
'I'm not going,' said Pete.
'I'll go,' said Mum.
'No, no, I'll go,' said Joe.
But it was too late. Mum was on her feet and heading for the front door like a battleship bearing down on a corvette. She flung it wide open to reveal, leaning against the door jamb, a small, wispy little bloke with a pencil-thin tash. He could have been an insurance salesman or a politician. He looked Mum over with a confident, sneering glance. Mum returned the look with interest. Oh no, I thought. It's the Man Next Door.
'Just what's going on these days in North . . . Ouch!'

He got no farther. Mum lifted him off his feet with her right hand and delivered a left hook that 'Our 'Enery' would have been proud of. His head snapped back and made violent contact with the wall, whereupon Mum let go of him and he slid to the ground like a sack of spuds. Mum pushed him off the doorstep with her slippered foot and slammed the door.

'I didn't like the look of him,' she said. 'Makes you wonder just what's going on these days in North Finchley.'

A few weeks later this large furniture van pulls up outside and all of a sudden the Man and Woman Next Door are next door no more.

I mustn't make you think that Mum was hooking people all the time. There were moments when she could be quite refined, although she made sure I never forgot my roots. She was a great leveller like that: the moment I let myself get up in the clouds, Mum could always be relied on to bring me down to earth – usually with a thud. On the other hand she wasn't above elevating me – or trying to elevate me – to what *she* considered was my rightful place in society when she thought it necessary.

A typical example would be when she was left in charge of the house while I was on tour. I'd ring up to see how she was getting on, only to get this posh voice saying, 'Helloo, *Mister* Brown's residence.'

'Come off it, Mum,' I used to tell her. 'You don't need to say that.'

If nothing else, I was scared my mates would think I was some sort of poser.

I sometimes wondered if being in the film had gone to her head. It was called *Spike Milligan meets Joe Brown* and it was the first film I ever did. It might have been the last, too, because I sussed straight from the off that the whole thing was going to take the mickey out of the whole rock and roll scene at the time. For a start, I didn't even get to meet Spike Milligan until eight or nine years after the film was finished – which made a nonsense of the title.

Of course it all came down to the Parnes in the beginning.

'You're going to do a film,' he told me one day.

'What's it called?' I asked.

'*Spike Milligan meets Joe Brown.*'

'Lovely,' I said. 'I like Spike Milligan.'

'Yes. We're all going to be in it.'

'What!' I exclaimed. 'You 'n' all?'

'Oh yes,' quoth he as if I'd offended him. 'I'll be in it. Jack Good'll be in it. I tell you, we'll all be in it and it'll be based around you.'

Filming Spike Milligan meets Joe Brown. *I'm talking to the producer, Gerry Bryant.*

Great, I thought. My name in lights from Clapton to Chelsea. But then we started filming and there was no sign of Spike Milligan. Someone asked me a lot of questions which I'd answer in front of the camera, and what happened was that the answers were mixed with a lot of different questions which Spike would ask and which made me look like an idiot. Very naughty! And they did it with everyone – Larry, Jack Good, the lot.

They had Larry taking a phone call.

'Say the sort of things you'd say in a business call,' they told him. So Larry picks up the phone on the set and starts off. 'Hello. (Pause.) Yes, yes. Course. (Pause.) Right. (Pause.) Yes. Quite right.' And so on. You could always rely on Larry to ham it up.

But when the film came out, Spike Milligan's voice was on the other end of the phone, asking things like, 'Is it true you fiddle all your boys?' And there was old Larry saying, 'Course. Right. Yes. Quite right.'

They had Jack Good smoking a cigarette and blowing the smoke into the air – but then they reversed the film so that the smoke was going back into Jack's mouth, and Spike's voice-over was saying, 'That's the thing about Jack Good. Never wastes anything.' It was a terrible thing to do, though I thought it was a great laugh at the time.

The best bit was when they came to the house 'to film a young pop star in his flat with his mum'. First of all the producer, Gerry Bryant his name was, began to brief Mum.

'What we want you to do, Mrs Brown, is walk in, say "Hello, Joe", go to the mantelpiece, pick up some papers from it, put them on the table and say "I'm going out shopping now. There are some letters from the office for you to sign, and if you want anything to eat" – you walk over to the fridge now and open the door – "there's some food in the fridge." Then you close the door and go out.'

He went over this a couple of times and we all got into position. Gerry says 'Action', the girl with the clapper does her Take one clap, and in storms Mum like Larry Olivier, Marlon Brando and Boris Karloff all rolled into one. She picks up the papers off the mantelpiece all right, but then, with her arms waving all over the place in grand dramatic gestures, she screams to me in this amazing posh voice. 'Joseph! There are some letters here for you to sign.' Down she goes on one knee and flings them across the coffee table. Then she's up again and rushing to the fridge, flinging the door open and gesticulating towards it with both hands. 'And there are some cheese sandwiches in here. I'm going out now.' Off she flounces, slamming the door behind her.

'Cut!' yells Gerry: and 'Take two' and 'Cut' and 'Take three' and so it went on all morning. 'Take fifty-six' and Mum's still going at it. The crew's in hysterics. Except for Gerry who's past seeing the funny side of it.

So years later, when I told her that there were some record and TV people coming to dinner, in the hope that I could tie up a record deal to go with the TV show we were negotiating, there was no keeping Mum away. But instead of just sitting there and being bloody picturesque in her duffel coat and M & S slippers, she had to keep getting up, fetching things and whipping people's plates away as soon as *she* thought they'd finished. She'd obviously caught the mood from the best crockery and crystal my wife Vicki had set to make a good impression, and in the absence of the Swedish au pair, Mum was determined to do her bit to show that the Browns knew how to go about things. When the phone rang, she was on her feet in a flash.

'I'll get it – son,' she said, wrenching the phone from the cradle.

Making another film, Three Hats for Lisa, *singing 'Operas and Oranges'.*

'Helloo,' she bawled in a loud voice just in case the call's long distance. 'Mister Brown's residence.'

Everybody turned to look at me. I felt embarrassed: I was embarrassed. I just had to say something. 'Now then, Mum,' I began, laughing weakly. 'You don't need to say that when you answer the phone.'

'Wasser matter wiv yer?' she said, waving the phone around and looking straight at me. 'I don't unnerstand yer 'tall. Yer want people ter fink you got a few bleedin' bob, doncha?'

I got the TV series – and the record deal. Thanks, Mum.

9 Parnes, shillings and pence

I worked for Larry Parnes for the best part of three years. There was the *Boy Meets Girls* TV show that Marty Wilde hosted, and after that *Wham*. Twice a year Larry's tours of the country with American stars like Del Shannon, Dion, Gene Vincent and Eddie Cochran; plus people like Billy Fury and Marty from Larry's stable. Great shows they were. Sometimes as many as fifteen or sixteen acts on the bill, unlike today when you get several hours of the same band. The big difference, of course, is that whereas we'd have paid to get on stage and play, today's rock stars have got it together better. They know what they're worth. We were getting something like sixteen quid a week in those days, regardless of whether we were on a TV show, a tour, or topping the bill at a ballroom in Grimsby. And we worked every night. Little wonder Larry could afford to put on shows with fifteen acts a night and bring over big names from America.

There were record sessions as well, but whenever I could I never let on to the Parnes about those. They were my perks. There was a time in the early 1960s when I had some success with my own records, like 'A Picture of You', written by Pete Oakman, but at the start I never thought of myself as a singer. I was the lead guitarist in a band full of hardened musicians, many of them from the Ted Heath Band and specially employed for the TV shows or the tours. Sometimes I wonder how I managed it, because I didn't think I was that good a musician. Later, thanks to working with people like Eddie Cochran, I developed a style and a sound – more of an American sound – of my own and that got me session work with Billy Fury, Adam Faith and their like.

The most important thing I learnt from Eddie Cochran was how to

Billy Fury, Jess Conrad, Gene Vincent, me, Eddie Cochran, Adam Faith and Marty Wilde rehearsing for Wham!

'bend' a note. In those days you'd buy a standard set of strings for your guitar; not like today when you buy a string according to whatever gauge you want; and I noticed that Eddie used a second string in place of the third. It was with this 'unwound third' that he produced the special elongated sound which can make a guitar so distinctive.

We first met in January 1960 when he came to England for the second series of *Boy Meets Girls* and to tour with Larry's 'Fast Moving Anglo-American Beat Show'. I was his lead guitarist on the tour and got to know him as well as you can get to know someone in a few months. He was a lovely guy to be on the road with, easygoing and full of fun, and as a musician he was great company because he was always playing. We'd sit up most nights, picking and strumming, and I suppose if anyone taught me to play the guitar, it was Eddie Cochran. At the same time I learnt what rock and roll was really all about – and the person who taught me was Gene Vincent.

Gene had come over to Britain in December to tape some songs for *Boy Meets Girls* and to do a series of dates in Europe before topping the bill on the Beat Show. Larry had the Oakmans and me down at Heathrow at six o'clock in the morning to greet him with 'Be-Bop-A-Lula', and the next day, a Sunday, we backed him on the Marty Wilde Show at the Tooting Granada – with hardly any rehearsal and almost any old equipment. Poor Albert Oakman had to drive all the way to Leyton and back for our amplifiers.

Working with Gene Vincent was a knockout. Literally. He had this crippled left leg as a result of a motorbike accident in 1955 when he was twenty. A car had gone through a red light and knocked him off his Triumph. The leg never healed properly throughout his life, and Gene was always breaking it and having it reset. Britt Hagarty, who interviewed me for a book he was writing on Gene,* told me that the leg had four metal screws in it and had sheep bone grafted on to it. The doctors had originally wanted to amputate it but Gene had begged them not to. By the time I met him it caused him no end of pain and he wore a metal brace to support it. How the hell he managed to swing it over the microphone I never knew. But he did. It was part of his act. Usually as a lead into 'Be-Bop-A-Lula', which is what he opened with this Sunday at the Tooting Granada. He limped on stage as we played him on, grabbed hold of the microphone, swung his left leg in a circle over the stand and cracked me on the side of the head. Talk about working with the stars – I was seeing them as well.

I've often wondered if Gene took to wearing black leather on stage as a result of working with me. Being motorbike mad in my early days I was often in black leather – on and off stage – and by the time we got to shooting the second series of *Boy Meets Girls*, Gene was into leather pants and jackets as well. The way he hunched over the microphone, dressed all in black, his crippled leg stretched out behind him, he was a magnetic presence – the epitome of the rock and roll rebel. And his singing was tremendous. It wasn't just the girls who went crazy over him. The blokes were in the aisles jiving: they loved him. No way would they hurl abuse and bottles at him the way they did some nights at poor old Billy Fury, who was also on the Anglo-American Beat Show with us.

The girls used to go wild when Billy was on stage: screaming and jumping all over the place. But their boyfriends: they'd come to see Gene Vincent. So while Billy was strutting his stuff, giving the chicks their big thrill for the night, the blokes were sitting there simmering and swearing. 'Bloody kill 'im' they were all threatening. Which made me glad my act was rock and roll and not sex. The blokes were usually on my side.

* *The Day the World Turned Blue*, Blandford Press, 1984.

Being motorbike mad during the early sixties I often wore black leather on and off stage.

There was one night, Billy came rushing out of the theatre intent on a quick getaway to find that the roadie hadn't unlocked the door of the car. Girls were grabbing bits of him and blokes were throwing punches at him. It was pandemonium. Billy put up an arm to protect himself and accidentally walloped some girl in the face. At which very moment there's a flash and some amateur photographer's racing down the street screaming 'Scoop! Scoop!' followed by a furious Billy, some rent-a-roadie, screaming girls and swearing fellas.

Gene, Eddie and I had a similar experience one night after a show at the Leeds Empire. We made it to the car all right, though. Hal Carter, the roadie, and Gene in the front, Eddie and me in the back, the empty road ahead, the screaming fans behind. But what happened? The lights turned red.

Next thing the front door's flung open. (Eddie and I have locked the back ones.) Gene's struggling, girls' hands are groping, and Eddie's shouting at Hal to get driving. After what seems an age we're off again and the crowd's been left behind. Eddie's telling Hal what a shit-awful driver he is when there's this wail from the front seat.

'Eddie' – all lost like. Whenever Gene was feeling lost, which was a lot of the time, he turned to Eddie. They were great pals.

'What is it, Gene?'

'They've got mah trousers, Eddie!'

And they had. The girls had whipped his leather trousers off him while he was sitting in the car, leaving him wearing just a black T-shirt, his Y-fronts, and that big metal brace around his withered white leg. Everybody stared when the four of us walked across the hotel foyer, and you could tell just what they were thinking.

It's hard to believe, thinking back on those days now, that both Eddie and Gene are dead. Eddie was killed just a month or so later, in April, when the car taking him to Heathrow crashed in Chippenham. He and Gene were about to fly back to the States for a holiday before resuming their British tour. Gene, though badly hurt, survived. Sort of. Emotionally he was in a bad way for a lot of the time from then until he died in 1971.

The time we all had together was brief, only a couple of months, but as a rock guitarist they were the most important, most inspirational months of my career.

Another American who had some effect on my career was Johnny Cash. Not on my playing but on my appearance. Yet working with him almost got me the sack from the TV show *Wham!*. We were recording in Manchester, but because the signals were being sent down telephone lines into an Ampex recording machine in London, the show might just as well have been live. The cost of Ampexing was so high that the producers never wanted to do more than one take and there was next to no editing.

For this particular show Johnny Cash was appearing on his own. That is, without The Tennessee Two, who were his backing group and not the only notes he sang. One of the Two was a very fine guitar player name of Luther Perkins, whose way of picking the strings note for note and blocking the sound with his hand achieved that donk dink, donk dink, donk dink sound which was a feature of Johnny Cash records. Johnny had told me this was how he wanted me to play and everything was fine. I could see myself making a fortune in Nashville if all you had to do all day long was go donk dink, donk dink, donk dink and call everybody Buddy. After all, Luther Perkins had once been a mechanic for the Automobile Sales Garage in Memphis.

So now we're recording and Johnny's singing 'How high's the water, momma?' and I'm a-going donk dink, donk dink, donk dink, doing my thing.

Playing with the band on the Boy Meets Girls *show. I'm wearing the cowboy boots Johnny Cash sent me.*

'Five feet high and rising' – donk dink, donk dink.

'How high's the water, poppa?' – donk dink, donk dink.

'Oh, you'll make it to the road, my son' – donk dink, donk dink.

But the water's getting higher, and I'm just about donk dinking myself to sleep up there. So halfway through the second verse I try a little do-wing dinga ding among the donk dinks: and Johnny Cash stops singing.

'Hold it,' he says, and there's this almighty hush. No one knows what's going on. This has never previously happened. No one's ever stopped the show before. The producer's coming on to the stage but all eyes are on Johnny. Slowly he turns from the front-stage mike and looks back towards the band until his eyes alight on me.

'Joe,' he drawls. 'Thar'll be no pickin' thar.'

Everybody stared at me. Then Johnny turned back to the mike and we took two. After the show they told me I wouldn't be required again:

but I was. I think Johnny must have put in a good word for me, and though I never did get to Nashville, I did get my boots. A couple of months after the show a letter arrived from HM Customs and Excise saying there was a parcel for me at their Hackney office which I had to collect some time.

They didn't say what was in it, and I had no idea. People had stopped sending food parcels years before. Still, nothing ventured nothing gained, they say, so I made my way down to Hackney. Perhaps I should've taken a cab but you get a better look into people's houses from the top of a bus. Besides, you don't have to tip the clippie. Well, you didn't in those days anyway.

The official who found my parcel looked a bit bored with life. Or he'd had a row with his wife. He hadn't even seen me on the telly. So I thought I'd cheer him up.

'Heard the story about the customs official who got nicked going home with the day's takings?' I asked.

The official looked blank.

'He thought it was his duty, mate!'

'You have to open the parcel, Mr Brown.'

Not even a smile. I opened the parcel and my jaw dropped. So did his. Inside the box were the most beautiful pair of cowboy boots you could ever want to see. Hand-tooled in genuine leather with pink, yellow, blue and green detail.

'To Joe the picker. From Johnny Cash' read the card.

'$200' read the price tag.

'Two hundred dollars!' said the customs official in something approximating to awe. It would've been more than a month's wages to him. He kept feeling the leather and looking at the boots.

'You'll have to pay duty on them, I'm afraid.' And he sounded genuinely sorry. My heart sank.

'No way, mate. I'm skint. Honest.'

'How much have you got on you?'

I turned out my pockets.

'Couple of bob, a quid note, a used bus ticket. And I need that to get home again.'

He thought for a moment.

'Tell you what,' he said. 'Put them on for a minute.'

May as well do what he says, I thought. Might be the only chance I get to wear them. They fitted beautifully.

'I've never seen anything like them,' said the customs bloke. 'Aren't they something? OK. Walk up and down a bit in them.'

I did so.

'Right,' he says, reaching for his form and his pen. 'One second-hand pair of boots. That'll be a quid duty.'

Great bloke. No sense of humour but a heart of gold. I look out for him every time I'm sneaking an extra packet of Marlboro through Heathrow, but I reckon he's still down at Hackney, waiting for smugglers coming up through the Marshes. I still have the boots. They're a bit the worse for wear but I've had some mileage out of them. For a while they were as much a trademark as my blond spiky hair and cockney singing.

My singing career began through Jack Good, even though I wasn't very keen on the idea. He got me doing things like 'Seven Little Girls' (sittin' in the back seat, kissin' and a-huggin with Fred), with the result that more people began to notice me. I was becoming more than a spiky head of hair and a bent note – for those who noticed that sort of thing. Next thing I knew Larry had signed me up to cut a record for Decca – I did a Doc Pomus and Mort Shuman number called 'People

With Jack Good on drums. It was he who came up with the name the Bruvvers.

Gotta Talk' – and suddenly I had to have a band. And the band had to have a name. Jack Good came up with that as well, though I suspect it was his way of getting one back on me. Very well spoken was Jack. Good school; Oxford afterwards. Just the type for someone like me to take the mickey out of. I quickly got into the habit of calling him 'bruv', because to a railwayman everyone's 'bruv' or 'brother'. It's the union thing, I guess. Only it annoyed Jack no end. I didn't see why the label couldn't just say Joe Brown: the Parnes was still sulking about Elmer Twitch and The Fidgets: and so it was up to Jack to come up with a good name.

'I have the answer,' he announced in Good Balliol English. 'We'll call the band The Bruvvers. No. His Bruvvers. They'll be Joe Brown and His Bruvvers.'

At first they weren't even me mates, let alone me bruvvers. Just a lot of session musicians got together for the record. But when I went on the road as a singer, I told Larry that I wanted my own band, people I could work with and be happy with. He wasn't keen. It meant more money. But eventually he agreed and I went straight round to see the Oakmans. They'd always been my mates and now they became my first Bruvvers. Pete played bass, Tony played rhythm, and we picked up drummers whenever we needed them – which was pretty often. Drummers and me just never got along.

'Listen, son,' said the Parnes to me the moment I opened my mouth on the subject of expenses, 'forget that for now. Something much more exciting. A good friend of mine, you know his name, Lionel Bart, he's written a song for you. A smash hit he says it is. We're going round to listen to it.'

At that very moment I'd sooner have had my expenses than ten smash hits by Lionel Bart, whom I'd always taken to be a real smart-Alec West End songwriter. But I was in for a surprise. He turned out to be quite the opposite.

'Come in, my boy, come in,' he greeted us in a thick East End Jewish accent. 'You wanta cuppa tea so soon, you shall have it. Some tea for this boy,' he told an office girl. 'Lovely boy you have here, Larry. A great talent. Please God I should be so lucky,' he said, going over to a piano and picking up a piece of paper that was sitting on it. As far as I could see it was covered in numbers.

'D'you know what I've got here, my son?' he asked Larry, waving the paper in his face. Larry looked blank. You'd have thought Lionel had just asked him for threepence to pay for my plastic cup of tea.

'It's a hit song, my son. A hit song or my dick's a banjo.'

Let's hope he's right, I thought. I'd hate to hear 'Swanee River' played on that.

'How does it go, Mr Bart?' I ventured to ask, being a lovely boy and all.

Lionel threw a hand in the air to command our attention, took a theatrical breath, looked at the paper and hurled himself into his performance.

'Three five eight. Three five eight.' Pause. A glance at the paper. 'Ten ten ten ten, eight nine eight seven.' He looked across at us. 'GREAT! GREAT! Isn't it GREAT!'

'I don't think much of the lyrics,' I said.

'You wait till you hear the words. They're GREAT!'

'What about the tune then?'

'What about the tune?' he echoed enthusiastically. 'What about the tune? Ah Larry. Your boy here. Such a lovely sense of humour. Such innocence.' He waved the sheet of paper at me. 'This *is* the tune, schmuck!'

He flung up the lid of the piano to reveal the keyboard. I couldn't believe it. Every key had a number stuck on it.

'Key of C,' he said, glancing at the paper and looking up at me. 'Key of C and it goes like THIS!'

He immediately attacked the piano, stabbing frantically with his right forefinger at the notes with corresponding numbers while waving the paper jubilantly aloft with his left hand.

Three five eight – E G C.

'Jellied eels, jellied eels,
Wobbling abaht like wonkey wheels.'

He rushed across to me.

'Bleedin' great, isn't it? Bleedin' great. Listen to the next lines.'

Back he dashed to the piano.

'Why d'yah frahn and look so sickly,
Slide 'em dahn yer froat an' quickly.'

He stopped, obviously overcome with emotion.

'And to finish . . .' – his voice hushed reverently, then rose – 'THE CHORUS!'

Down came his right forefinger.

'DON'T BRING UP IN THE EMPTY CUP
THOUGH I KNOWS JUST 'OW YER FEELS.
WHEN YER GETS THE TASTE,
YER WON'T WANNA WASTE,
THOSE LUVVERLY JELLIED EELS.

'BLEEDIN' GREAT! BLEEDIN' GREAT!'

And to emphasize this conclusion he crashed down the lid of the piano. 'What d'you think, my boy?'

I was opening my mouth to say something when Larry burst in.

'It's great. What can I say? It's great. He'll record it next week.'

Which I did, and I'm pleased to say that good old Lionel wasn't such a mug after all. Come to that, neither was old Parnesy, but then he always was good when it came to money matters. That's why he was known to most of us as Parnes, shillings and pence. The pounds he could be very generous with (sometimes) and completely the opposite with the pennies (always). Which is the reason I'd gone to his office that morning about my expenses. Getting them out of him, especially after you'd been on the road, was usually a bit of a game.

The system was that you took your receipts for petrol, digs, food, etc. to Larry's office, where he went through them and, depending how he felt, would either pay you straightaway or try to knock you down. With me it was nearly always the latter.

'What's this?' he'd ask, waving a dirty scrap of paper at me.

'It looks like a receipt for a taxi from Euston to the office,' I'd reply on closer inspection.

'But it's not signed,' he'd howl in a tone full of pain.

'Larry,' I'd say in a voice equally pained, 'you try getting a taxi driver to take you, the group and all the gear anywhere, especially when it's pissing with rain, let alone asking him to sign a receipt for ten bob.'

There followed a stunned silence.

'Ten bob!' he screamed. 'Ten bob!'

'Actually,' I said, trying to placate him, 'it was nine bob. But I gave the bloke a shilling tip.'

Larry's face went purple.

'A shilling!' His voice went up two octaves. 'A shilling!'

There was a frightening pause, then he brought his fist crashing down on the desk, dislodging a framed picture of Johnny Gentle which fell to the floor and shattered.

'Threepence!' he shrieked. 'Threepence is quite sufficient.'

That was Larry. Look after the pennies and the lads could look after

Touring with the Bruvvers in the early days, playing at a typical ballroom.

themselves. And most of the time we had to, especially on the road. On tour wasn't so bad because we were all together in a coach and the accommodation was all set up. But when it was just you and the band in a van with all the gear, doing one-night gigs in ballrooms, it was a different story. There were supposed to be arrangements made so that you could pick up some money at different towns, but half the time you'd get there and be told the same old story.

'Sorry lads, no cash but there'll be a cheque in the post.'

One of the great show business lies.

Being stuck in the middle of nowhere with no money, no digs and no grub is no joke, and that's why a lot of bands and groups resorted to all kinds of fiddles to get by. For example, there was 'doing a runner', which is exactly what it sounds like. You'd go into a caff, eat your egg, bacon, sausage, chips, beans, tomatoes and fried bread – known in the trade as a full house – and as soon as everyone had finished you'd all get up together and run like hell. It was a bit rough pelting down the road belching up bits of fried bread with a dirty great ex-lorry driver breathing down your neck, but it beat singing abaht luvverly jellied eels on an empty stomach. On the other hand there were more subtle methods, such as the 'I only had a cup o' tea, guv' routine. It went like this.

First you'd find a caff where the cash desk was at the door and you paid on your way out. Then one of the band would go in, sit at an empty table and order a good full house from the waitress. When he was three-quarters of the way through his nosh, one of the other lads would go in and sit at the same table, taking care to ignore the other one completely. As the waitress took his order he'd chat her up a bit so that she'd remember him, and he'd ask for just a cup of tea. Both of them would finish at the same time, and when the first lad asked for his bill for the food, the other would ask for his for the cup of tea. As soon as she'd gone, the first bloke would pick up the bill for the cup of tea, go to the desk, pay and walk out. The second bloke always waited for another minute or so, lighting up a fag or doing something to pass the time, before taking the food bill to the till. When he was charged for the food, he'd act a bit taken aback and complain. Then he'd ask to see the manager. You always go to the top, even in the dingiest caff.

''Scuse me,' he'd say. 'This ain't my bill. I only had a cup o' tea, guv.'

The waitress would verify this and that was that. It never failed. Down the road it would be his turn to eat.

10 Billy Cotton's Band Show

When I was a boy, everybody knew Billy Cotton. He was the bloke who got up at half past twelve on a Sunday lunchtime and greeted the day with a loud 'Wakey, wakey' dead on one o'clock. To me, though, he was just a noise in the background while I tried to find the tanners among the winkle shells. I never dreamed that a day would come when I'd not only get to meet him but actually work with him.

I can't remember the exact year, but I recall getting a phone call from the Parnes to say he'd booked me on *Billy Cotton's Band Show*. I went mad.

'You must be joking,' I said, playing the big-headed pop star. 'That's corny.'

And corny it was, but not in the way I've come to think of things as corny. Corn, to me, has come to mean the custard pie that everyone knows is coming. But in the hands of people like Billy Cotton, corn can be an art. They get away with it. Professional comedians put it down to timing, and to a certain extent they're right. But it goes beyond timing. There has to be some human feeling there as well: a warmth that in people like Billy challenges them to try something on, to say something 'corny'. And because they have this warmth, they get away with saying things and doing things which, without their human touch, would not be funny.

In essence, they're 'trying to get to know you', and this was apparent in Billy when I first met him. A big man, in size as well as reputation, with a bald head and an earthy East End sense of humour, he struck me as the sort who felt himself responsible for everyone who came into contact with him. People in show business had the greatest respect for

The great Billy Cotton.

him, and that's saying something. They may not have all liked him, but I've never heard a word spoken of him that didn't have an undertone of respect. Like Ted Mead, he was one of the few gentlemen I've met, and to me he represented everything I would call real in this very dicey game called show business. After I'd been a regular guest on the *Band Show* for several years, Billy extended an open invitation to me to come along any time I had a record or something to plug. He always seemed pleased to have me on the show, and I made some very good friends through him. The whole *Band Show* team were some of the nicest people I've met.

One of those was Alan Breeze, or Breezy as he was known on the show. The funny thing about Breezy was that he had the most terrible stutter, yet on the *Band Show* he was the one who sang all the tongue-twisters. When he was in the role of one of his characters he was OK, but the moment he became himself again and got involved in a serious conversation he was reduced to a gibbering wreck.

Breezy had a pub in Flixton, Norfolk, called the Buck Inn. His beer mats carried the legend 'Don't pass the Buck'. As well as the pub he had a small farm, on which were some small cottages which he'd let to holidaymakers. I rented one for the summer once when I was doing a season at the Windmill Theatre in Great Yarmouth, and every night after the show I'd go back to Flixton and straight into the pub, where I'd sit with Alan sinking White Worthingtons until the wee small hours.

Many was the night I'd arrive to be greeted by Breezy in one of his Scottish characters. It would be 'Och noo the laddy' and such like until he got fed up with it and went back to stammering again. Or he'd break into Irish and chop and change all night until he'd exhausted his enormous repertoire. One time we were having a serious chat about fishing. Breezy worked his way through his accents and we were getting along fine on baits and tackle. But when he came to the end of his Chinaman (with a lisp) I knew he'd had it. His face went red and the veins in his neck stood out like a ruptured haggis.

'I bbbb-bought a f-ff-fishing rod once,' he said, 'from that lll-little sss-shop in Bbbbb . . .' he gestured with his arm in the direction of the town just past Flixton. 'Bbbbb . . .'

'Bungay,' I volunteered.

'Dddddd-don't bloody help me,' screamed Breezy.

11 On the road

Being on the road was a great apprenticeship as far as self-survival was concerned. People got used to handling situations that in any other sort of job they'd never find themselves in. And it was also a lot of fun.

One evening we arrived in a north of England town with half an hour to spare before the show was due to start. None of us had slept in a bed the night before. For breakfast we'd nicked the cream off the top of the milk churns when the farmer left them for collection. Somewhere off the A1 we'd managed a couple of runners and one 'I only had a cup o' tea, guv'. But that evening we were in luck. The cheque wasn't just in the post. There was some money for us at the theatre. That meant a bed for the night – if we could find one. We knew from past experience that we'd have to find somewhere to stay before the gig started. These towns were like ghost towns after eight o'clock. Only the vampires were out – and half of them had left their teeth in a glass by the coffin.

Leaving the others to unload the van – after all, they'd be sleeping in it – the Bass Player and I went round knocking on a few doors. No luck. It was getting late. Then we found a pub called the George and Dragon with a card in the window.

'Rooms to let. No dogs.'

That let the Drummer out.

The Bass Player knocked. No reply. I knocked. Still no reply. We knocked together: Bee bop a loo bop a lum bang bang. In C.

Six and a half minutes later the door opened and the ugliest woman I've ever seen poked her head around the door. One eye stared at the Bass Player's shoes and the other stared at the top of my head – both at the same time.

Poor woman, I thought.

'What d'you bleedin' want!' she screamed.

Instantly neutralizing my sympathy.

'D'you think the lady next door would give us a drink of water?' asked the Bass Player, using the old stock joke.

She glared at him with one eye and at a pigeon flying overhead with the other. Obviously she'd heard it before.

'Don't waste me bleedin' time,' she growled. 'I 'aven't got all day. Whadda ya want?'

'Excuse us,' I said, trying not to look at the wart on her nose. 'We're desperate for somewhere to stay' (we must have been) 'and we saw your card.'

'How much d'ya wanna pay?' she squawked.

'Fiver?' I asked, having already made up my mind.

She opened the door a bit and I got a quick look under her armpit into the inner sanctum. There wasn't much to see. Just a flight of stairs and, halfway up, on the landing, a huge Alsatian dog gnawing the biggest bloody bone I've ever seen.

'Five pounds between us,' I said quickly, showing her the note. Her left eye narrowed greedily. The right eye hadn't seen it yet.

'Awright.' She snatched the money. 'But I'll 'ave ter get the room ready first.'

That suited us fine. We were already late for the show, so we dumped our cases in the hall and left. When we got back, the pub was in darkness. We tossed a coin to see who was going to knock on the door, and I lost. It was my coin as well.

The standard six and a half minutes passed then the door was opened by a mild-mannered-looking man in striped pyjamas and tartan slippers with little bunny rabbits on the front.

'Can I help you?' he whispered.

I breathed a sigh of relief. This must be George.

'We're staying in the room,' I told him.

'Oh. Yes. You must be the two' – he looked around for the right word – 'gentlemen that Popsie said was to have the top room. Please follow me.'

He made his way up the stairs, mumbling 'Mind the bones,' and eventually we came to a short, dimly lit corridor leading off to the left and upwards. At the end of this he opened a door.

'Here we are, boys.'

No sooner were we inside than he shut the door behind us.

As rooms go it was all right. Nice and clean with two single beds (thank God) and a white kidney-shaped dressing-table with gold plastic edgings. A blue Polynesian lady with big tits leered at us from above a tiled gas fireplace, while a trio of plaster ducks winged their way to Lord knows where. It was the original Holiday Inn. Once seen, never forgotten.

But it was clean and we were knackered. We chucked off our clothes and dived into the beds. Last one in turned off the light. Only I was so tired I couldn't sleep. I tried counting sheep and that just had me nodding off when the bloody Bass Player started to snore.

'Jesus Christ!' I exclaimed.

'What's the matter with you?' came the immediate reply.

'You. Snoring.'

'Wasn't me. I've been awake all the time. I thought it was you.'

'I've been awake all the time too.'

'Then who was it?'

We listened. There it was again. Definitely someone snoring.

'Bloody hell,' I said. 'These walls must be thin.'

'Walls be buggered,' he declared. 'It's coming from this room.'

We both lay there frozen still, wondering what to do next. After all, neither of us was twenty yet. We could restring a guitar, change a wheel, scrounge a meal, but life hadn't prepared us for snoring ghosts.

'One of us better turn on the light,' decided the Bass Player, pulling the sheet over his head.

'Chicken,' I said, wondering if I was talking to him or me. I got up and turned on the light. There was nothing to be seen.

'Listen. There it is again.'

Sure enough, someone was snoring. I tried to locate the sound. It seemed to be coming from the cupboard in the corner, one of those tall, narrow alcoves by the chimney breast that had been faced with a flush hardboard door. I tiptoed across and pulled it open – very cautiously. The Bass Player peered over my shoulder.

We looked. And looked again. I couldn't believe my eyes. He couldn't believe his eyes. There, squatting in a foetal position, facing each other, their foreheads almost touching, were two old men, wrapped up in blankets and raincoats. One of them had a red and white striped woolly bobble cap on his head so he must have been a Sunderland supporter. They were both sound asleep.

'What're we going to do?' I asked.

'I don't know about you, mate,' replied the Bass Player, 'but I'm going to get some kip.'

I closed the door gently and went back to bed. In the morning the men had gone.

Later, chatting to a couple of locals in the pub, I learnt that the two old boys were permanent residents and Popsie had given them the boot for the night in favour of a couple of scruffy-looking rockers with a not-so-scruffy-looking five-pound note. The rotten old cow.

I often wonder what happened to those two old men. Maybe that bloody Alsatian got them.

12 Terry and the Teds

We were ripping up a storm playing 'Johnny B. Goode' when I saw the balcony bouncing. It scared the life out of me. I couldn't take my eyes off it. It was going up and down a matter of inches in time to the music. More to the point, in time to the fans stomping their feet in time to the music. To me at the time it was the most frightening thing I'd seen. I sometimes lay awake at night imagining what would happen if a balcony collapsed, because the cinemas and theatres we played in weren't built for people to dance and stomp to the beat in. Even soldiers, someone once told me, broke step when marching across a bridge to avoid setting up a rhythm that could damage the structure. Yet here were these Teddy boys setting up just such a vibration every time a rock and roll show came to their local Odeons, Hippodromes, Empires and Granadas.

Trying to bring the house down unintentionally didn't stop the Teds smashing it up by more conventional means as well. Like the night of the Terry Dene riot. I've already mentioned elsewhere that a lot of the blokes didn't take kindly to pelvis-swinging singers getting their girls all worked up – especially as getting worked up was what the girls went along for. As a result the sex-image singers got a rough time, and when it became known that Terry Dene had got out of doing his National Service, that made him an even bigger target.

Remember National Service? Lots of silly buggers running round playing soldiers on Salisbury Plain. Very healthy, they say. They talk about bringing it back but they never do. Marty Wilde got out of doing National Service, so he told me, because he had flat feet. And if you ever saw them you knew he wasn't pulling your leg. His cobbler used a spirit level. But poor old Terry Dene. He avoided it because he had a

An early playbill from the Tooting Granada.

nervous breakdown. Not the best of reasons when you're shaking your hips in front of a crowd of Teds who've just put in eighteen months' square-bashing. Especially if their girlfriends are flooding weepies all over their best drapes and rusting their fish hooks.

Fish hooks were a must for the heavy-mob Teds. Otherwise the equipment was standard for all of them: the drape suit with the velvet collar, jacket regulation finger-tip length, bootlace tie, drainpipe trousers (blue jeans acceptable in some quarters) and blue suede shoes. The hair slicked back to a DA that kissed the velvet collar and a quiff solid with Brylcreem bobbing away at the front. To see them doing their regulation walk put you in mind of a motorway crow.

The fish hooks, for those who wore them, were sewn behind the lapels, so when the action got rough in the ballroom on a Saturday night anyone grabbing the Ted by his coat was suddenly transfixed. Whereupon it was a blue suede shoe scraped down the shin, a quick knee in the groin and a violent blow between the eyes from the lethal quiff. All that anyone could do was hang on and hope that the band played a waltz.

The time of the Terry Dene riot, though, a waltz was not the answer. There was violence in the air that night and we could feel it when we were doing our set. The management could feel it, too, because when the show finished they kept us inside the theatre, on the stage, waiting until the crowd outside began to disperse. Only it didn't. Some people drifted off, but from where we were we could hear the Teds yelling what they were going to do to Terry once they got their hands on him. Not very nice, as the Parnes would say.

Just when we thought it was getting quiet, the lull was broken by a shattering crash on the iron scene-dock door (where the stage scenery is taken in and out of the theatre). The Teds had broken down a telegraph pole and were using it as a battering-ram. I don't know which was worse, the crash of wood on metal as they hit the door or the silence as they moved back for their next attempt. Talk about siege conditions. I was shaking in my shoes, unable to decide if I was more worried about my skin or my guitars. I was still only nineteen or twenty and had yet to get my priorities sorted out. Then the police arrived and it was pandemonium. Dogs, truncheons, whistles, fish hooks, bent quiffs, lord knows what. It was worse than feeding time at the House of Commons.

In Scotland, of course, the audiences don't even wait till the show is over if they don't like you. There's a thin line there between an audience and a mob: as Screaming Lord Sutch discovered one night. Fortunately we weren't playing with him. In fact, any night we weren't playing with him was fortunate, because apart from getting up to these outrageous stunts like coming on stage strapped to a cross, he was a great stage-wrecker. He did terrible things like pouring paraffin over the piano and setting fire to it. That's why if ever we were on the same bill, I always insisted on going before him. Nine times out of ten if you went after him there'd be no stage left!

On this occasion, Lord Sutch was doing a two-nighter at a ballroom in Scotland. As always he was got up in some outrageous gear, and of course with him there was never anything as simple as walking straight on stage as the group played his entrance music. Oh no. Sutchie had to make his entrance from the back of the ballroom and walk through the crowd. Only this night one of the Jocks in the audience took a dislike to him and hit him: a recreation quickly taken up by the other Jocks and Teds in the audience. So by the time he reached the stage, his amazing gear was all in tatters. Even worse, his own band were standing there laughing at him!

Next night, backstage, he dressed in another of his amazing outfits, but as soon as the band went up front, he quickly changed back into his street clothes, took off all his make-up, and rushed round the hall to the main entrance, slipping in unrecognized and standing among the audience at the back of the ballroom. Up on stage the band were playing away, every now and then looking into the crowd to see why Sutchie still hadn't given his cue. On and on they played, and the audience began to get restless. The more they muttered and shouted abuse, the more ragged the band played. Finally Sutchie could take no more. He played his card.

'What a bloody awful band,' he screamed at the top of his voice. 'Let's get 'em!'

Whereupon the Jocks rushed the stage and beat up the band. Sutchie went home with honour satisfied.

The only trouble I had in Scotland was not with the audience but with my drummer, a lad called Tommy Brown who'd played for a time with Johnny Duncan and the Bluegrass Boys and later with Nero and the Gladiators. I was waiting in the wings while the band were playing the warm-up and it suddenly got through to me that there was no drumming. Actually it didn't sound too bad without it, but I mean, you've got to have a drummer if there's a drum kit on the stage. Sorry, I digress. Anyway, next thing I knew, there was Tommy walking off the stage, saying things like 'That's it, man. I'm quitting. I'm no good. They're all laughin' at me.' And so on.

Now Tommy did have a big inferiority complex, but to me it was a plain case of a guy who'd lost his bottle. So I gave him a righthander around the nut and he was as good as gold. Went back out and did a terrific set. Come to think of it, it wasn't so much that he'd lost his bottle as that he'd found one: as I discovered after the show when I sat him down for a little heart to heart.

'That's it then, mate. No more drinking's the answer,' I told him.

But the next night was Hogmanay. What a time to give up the demon drink! Yet he was good about it, keeping on the orange juice while the rest of us were knocking back pints in the pub before the show. Coming out of the pub, I noticed this drunk weaving down the street with a bottle of whisky in his hand, so I said to the Bass Player, 'Let's not get mixed up with him. We'll cross over.'

Tommy, however, had gone to the loo – all that orange juice – and came out just as the bloke was passing the door of the pub.

'Sorry, mate,' we heard him say as he bumped into the bloke.

'Have a drink, Jimmy,' said the Scotsman.

Tommy looked across to where the Bass Player and I were waiting.

'Sorry, mate. Got to work.'

He started to move but the bloke grabbed his jacket with one hand and thrust the bottle towards him with the other.

'Have a drink, Jimmy,' he growled.

'No offence, mate, but I'm not allowed to. I gotta work tonight.'

'Wasser matter with yer, Jimmy? It's Hogmanay. Are yer tellin' me yer won't have a drink with me on Hogmanay, yer bloody little Sassenach?'

Whereupon the Scotsman hit him with the bottle. Poor old Tommy, done over one night because he'd been drinking and done over the next because he wouldn't. It could only happen to a drummer.

13 On tour

'I want you to compere the show this afternoon.'

'Why me?' I asked.

'Because,' replied the Parnes, 'you've always got a lot to say for yourself. Now's your big chance.'

'But I've never done it before, have I?'

'History, my boy. Just think, by this evening you'll have done it twice.'

'What's it worth then?'

'You can have your own spot.'

'I've already got my own spot.'

'You see how generously I treat you. Yet I ask you one small favour and what do I get? Arguments.'

I gave up. After all, it was no big deal, compering a show. You just chat up the audience for a few minutes while the next band set up their kit. Or so I thought. It looked easy when the usual compere did it, but he'd gone sick and looked like being sick for most of the tour. It was a show called Idols on Parade, with people like Tommy Bruce and Mark 'Venus in Blue Jeans' Wynter.

First afternoon in front of the curtain I did the old customs officer gag. Stick to familiar material, I told myself. But what happens when I get to the punchline? The whole bloody audience yells,

'HE THOUGHT IT WAS HIS DUTY!'

No one had told me the audience contained two coachloads of customs officials on an afternoon outing to Blackpool.

It was obvious I needed a new routine. It was also obvious I needed a new manager and a new joke but there wasn't time to do anything

TODAY'S PROGRAM

LARRY PARNES presents

IDOLS ON PARADE!

Produced by JACK GOOD

Associate Producer: LESLIE COOPER — Stage Director: WIN NEWPORT — Musical Direction: SYD DALE

Featuring 1960's Top Recording Stars

JOE BROWN - TOMMY BRUCE - BILLY FURY
DAVE SAMPSON - VINCE EAGER - NELSON KEENE
DUFFY POWER - DICKIE PRIDE - JOHNNY GENTLE
PETER WYNNE - GEORGIE FAME - DAVY JONES
JOHNNY GOODE - THE VISCOUNTS - BILLY RAYMOND
RED PRICE with JIMMY NICOL and his 15 NEW ORLEANS ROCKERS

1. The public may leave at the end of the performance or exhibition by all exit doors and such doors must at that time be open. 2. All gangways, corridors, staircases and external passage-ways intended for exit shall be kept entirely free from obstructions whether permanent or temporary. 3. Persons shall not be permitted to stand in any of the gangways intersecting the seating, or to sit in any of the other gangways. If standing be permitted in the gangways at the sides and rear of the seating, it shall be limited to the number indicated in the notices exhibited in those positions. 4. Safety curtains must be lowered and raised in the presence of the audience.

about either right then. The other problem I had was knowing when the lads behind the curtain were ready to start their act. It was all very well the Parnes saying it was five minutes maximum or whatever between acts. *I* couldn't keep looking at my watch or poking me head round the corner asking 'Are you lot ready yet?' So I devised a set of cue lines with the various artists: usually tying something in with their first number. It worked fairly well until one afternoon when one of the mikes went duff just as I was about to introduce Tommy Bruce.

Tommy's opening number was 'Great Balls of Fire', the Jerry Lee Lewis hit, and his cue to let me know he was ready was to interrupt my front-of-stage patter with a cry of 'Fire! Fire!' through an off-stage mike.

'Fire?' I'd say. 'Where?'

And I'd run off in search of it. Immediately Tommy would leap on stage, grab my mike, yell 'Great Balls of Fire' and the band would set off.

Boom boom boom boom – 'You shake my nerves and you rattle my brain . . .' Too much of Parnes drives a man insane.

Touring with Idols on Parade.

Tommy Bruce is away and Joe Brown takes his breather.

This afternoon in Blackpool, though, Tommy's off-stage mike didn't work, with the result that the audience didn't hear his 'Fire! Fire!' Suddenly I stop in the middle of some gag, say 'Fire? What fire? Where?' and run off stage. OK. Tommy's on straight away and the penny drops for most of the audience. But there's this twit who doesn't know his Jerry Lee from his Peggy Lee and he's legging it to the front of the house shouting 'Fire! Fire! The theatre's on fire.' Next thing you know, ten and twenty firemen come bursting through the back of the theatre with hosepipes and axes at the ready. End of show. They wouldn't let us continue. Emptied the theatre. Poor old Tommy never even finished his song. The Parnes begged and blustered, cajoled and carried on, even threatened to phone his MP except she was on holiday. It was ever so funny.

The way I saw it, it was Parnsey's own fault for making me the compere in the first place. And I'd got my own back after the business with the suit . . .

The suit was a red and yellow number which was part of my act. Red down one side of me and yellow down the other side. Even the tie was in different colours down each half. The idea was that half of me would appear from the stage-left wings in red, I'd start a song or whatever, and during the instrumental I'd nip round to stage-right, where the yellow half would finish off the number. It was rock and roll, but in some ways it was still variety.

There was a law that said if we did a show on Sundays costumes could not be worn: only street clothes. An inspector would come into the theatre to check on what everyone was wearing, and of course as soon as he saw my suit he ruled it out of court. Not my Sunday best, he considered.

'But he wears it all the time,' argued Larry in the suit's defence. 'You know what these kids are like. They wear anything to attract attention.'

'I'll believe it when I see it,' said the inspector.

You'll see it all right, my son, thought Larry, hot-footing it for the dressing-room. Next thing I knew I was spending every free moment of the day walking up and down the sea-front in this red and yellow suit. A right prat I felt, I can tell you.

A kind of madness seems to take hold of you when you're on tour for any length of time. Everyone's read stories of famous pop singers and rock musicians smashing up hotel rooms just for the hell of it. This kind of behaviour came to prominence with bands like The Who and the Stones, and I couldn't even attempt to explain the whys and wherefores of it. Maybe it was just frustration at being away from home for long lengths of time, living out of suitcases and having virtually no privacy at all. It's bad enough being confined to a hotel room, but after a while all hotel rooms look the same and you begin to hate them. Physically hate them.

At one time, causing havoc in hotels was quite the thing to do. Then, at the end of the stay, the tour manager would settle the bill for the damage. This became so much the norm that lots of hotels, particularly in America, looked forward to the arrival of some of the richer rock bands. It was the only way they could get the place redecorated.

I heard a story about one band whose bill ran into thousands of dollars just for the damage they caused. Even the tour manager was embarrassed and wanted to give the hotel manager a nice big tip. He refused it, saying, 'I don't know why you guys do this, but I'd sure like to do it myself sometimes.'

'Be my guest,' said the tour manager. 'Just put it on the bill.'

Don't run away with the idea, though, that this all started with the heavy rock bands of the late sixties and seventies. I have it on good authority that such favourites as Jim Reeves and Johnny Cash got up to all sorts of things on tour. The story has it that Johnny once sat in his bath while his roadies filled it brim-full of quick-set jelly. Whereupon Johnny called the hotel manager to his room and complained.

'Thar's something wrong with this har water.'

As far as tours went, I don't think the boys and I ever did any real damage. None that we had to pay for, that is. We usually managed to blame it on someone else. But when it came to madness we were top of the list, on stage or off. Billy Fury used to do a number called 'Old Shep': the sort of song that gives a dog a bad name. To say it was sentimental would be too big a favour. So one night, when he was singing about poor old Shep, the boys and I took some off-stage mikes into the toilets, and when Billy came to the really weepy bit we pulled the chains. You couldn't say Billy was flushed with the success of that little prank. Pissed off would be more like it.

That was nothing, though, to some of the things we got up to on the Rock and Trad Shows: big touring shows at the beginning of the Sixties, directed by Jack Good with Larry putting up the money, I suppose. The Rock and Trad Show was the first big-production rock show of its kind and opened at the old Metropolitan theatre in London's Edgware Road. All in all it was a proper, well-organized extravaganza, quite unlike the usual cocked-up production.

The band – orchestra if you like – comprised some of the finest musicians of the time, most of them hardened jazz players from the top London big bands, with a smattering of just-graduated skifflers like myself thrown in. It was something like a twenty-piece band in all. Then there were sixteen dancers, the Valentine Girls and more than enough singers: names like Billy Fury, Georgie Fame, Vince Eager, The Four Kestrels, Davey Jones and many many more. Everyone in the band was dressed in some sort of costume. Andy White, one of the drummers, was dressed as a burglar; the musical director on one of the shows, Sid Dale, was done up like Sherlock Holmes with a deerstalker hat and large cape; one of the trumpet players, a dour moustachioed Scot called Dickie McPherson, was a belly dancer; and so on. I was dressed in a heavy tweed suit and a brown bowler hat, but I insisted on wearing my cowboy boots. I must have looked a twerp.

Because of the organizational problems of touring such a large company, I didn't have my own group with me, so Jack put me on guitar in the orchestra and gave me a couple of songs to sing during the show, plus a small spot of my own towards the end. However, as on the television shows, I had a hard time getting through to the professional musicians from outside the rock and roll world. Most of them just didn't want to know me, and if they did speak, you got the feeling that they suffered you only because they had to. Their sense of humour was different, too, based heavily on sarcasm. They gave the impression that nothing could ever rattle them – and I became more and more determined to put this to the test.

I remembered something my mum had told me about how Dad was forever having his lunchbox raided by the farm labourer he was working alongside. So he bought a large bar of laxative chocolate and rewrapped it inside the paper of a bar of Bournville. That cured him, Mum said; he never raided the old man's lunchbox again. However, there was no way I could pull this one on a bunch of super-cool musicians. They'd spot the difference straight away.

Feen-a-mint. That was the answer. Feen-a-mint was a laxative chewing gum, exactly the same size and shape as a well-known brand of chewing gum called Beechnut. How was I going to administer it? I let Vince Eager into the plan and the two of us went out and bought a dozen packets of each. We removed the Beechnut from their packets and refilled them with the Feen-a-mint, all except for the top one in each packet. The next stage was to open a packet in front of someone, pop the Beechnut into your mouth, start chewing and wait for the inevitable 'Give us a bit, you greedy bastard.'

Being generous of spirit we usually handed over the rest of the packet, which with any luck was then shared around. It worked every time. The gag *and* the Feen-a-mint. I suppose you could say it was the show's running gag for a couple of days.

Oh yes. I forgot to mention. We also nailed up the toilet doors beforehand. But then, as I said to Vince at the time, it wasn't as if we'd forced anyone to take a piece, was it?

It was the Feen-a-mint that gave rise to the shooting incident: another gag but much more subtle. Mind you, it had to be. No one was going to get caught again – or so they thought.

Winding people up is an art usually acquired only after years of being caught out yourself – mostly by musicians, who claim to be the best at it. It requires a great deal of planning, timing and credibility. Which means it's much easier if you have one or two accomplices: carefully chosen, of course, because the last thing you want is a giggler who can't keep a straight face. I found just the right person in Roger Greenaway of The Four Kestrels vocal group. Like just about everyone on the show Roger had suffered the gallops, so it came as no surprise to anyone to hear us shouting the odds about it one day. The thing was, we didn't let it stop there.

That night we were in Vince Eager's dressing-room and Vince produced this .38 revolver, a very large, evil-looking piece, which had been modified to fire blanks.

'How many people know you've got this?' I asked him.

'No one,' he said. 'I ain't supposed to have it.'

I couldn't believe my luck.

'Right,' I said. 'Start showing it around to a few people you know can't keep their mouths shut. But don't tell 'em it only fires blanks.'

'You'll get me bloody nicked,' Vince protested.

'Not if you're careful. Anyway, it'll be worth it. If Rog and me can keep this argument going, we can wind the lot of them up to such a pitch that when I shoot him no one'll be surprised. Just think of their faces. I can see 'em now. I bet half of them won't need Feen-a-mint.'

There were four or five of us in the dressing-room and we were all in on it. Roger was over the moon about the idea. A little bloke with a cheeky face and a slight twitch in his left eye, he was a great favourite with everyone on the tour because he always seemed to be winking at them. The girls in the chorus were especially fond of him, apart from one called Shirley who never gave him a second look. For the next couple of days we kept up the row. I'd go storming into his dressing-room shouting abuse and threatening him with all sorts of things, then tear out again, slamming the door and swearing I'd kill him, so help me. In the coach travelling between shows, he'd go round telling people nasty stories about me until eventually things were really getting out of hand. Everybody on the tour had taken sides. The atmosphere was electric.

Saturday night was to be the night. But when? It had to be where everybody could witness it, and the only time that everybody was on stage together was at the end of the finale. We laid our final plans. And just before curtain-up that night we came to blows in the corridor. No one actually hit anyone, but Vince did a great job holding me back, while Rog was similarly restrained by the other lads who were in on it. Even some of the musicians tried to calm us down: and when I saw this I knew we were going to get them.

During the interval we started up again: me accusing him of tuning down my guitar and trying to make me look a fool: him saying I wouldn't know if it was in tune or not, at which point I went off my head. We were both ushered to our rooms by the near-frantic stage manager, who by this time was beginning to foam at the mouth. The second half went off all right – until we got to The Four Kestrels' spot, when I played a couple of really bum chords in one of their songs. On purpose. The Musical Director shot me a terrible look which I ignored completely.

At last the finale arrived. I don't mind saying I was beginning to wonder if we'd gone too far, but it was too late to turn back now. Down came the curtain, and no sooner were we cut off from the audience than Roger, in front of everyone, started shouting about amateur guitar players. That was my cue. I dashed from the stage, scattering people as I went, and raced straight up the stairs to Vince's dressing-room for the gun. I was back on stage just as they were all turning to make their way off.

I don't think anyone else saw the gun until I raised it and shot him. Right between the eyes. Roger, who had a small shampoo sachet filled with tomato sauce taped to his hand, clapped his hand to his forehead (so squashing the sachet), threw himself backwards and crashed against the heavy safety curtain that had just been lowered. The effect frightened even me – and I was prepared for it. I can honestly say that nobody moved or said a word for at least fifteen seconds. A long time when you think about it. I looked around at their faces. They were white. Two girls fainted. And all those super-cool musicians just stood there shaking. A stage-hand was the first to speak.

''E's only bleedin' shot 'im,' he said.

Pandemonium broke out. Two people ran for the police and an ambulance (Vince stopped them at the stage door), girls were screaming and crying, and surly Shirley the chorus girl rushed to Roger and cradled his head in her arms. (Thank God she didn't try to kiss his bloody wound.)

'Roger, Roger,' she crooned. 'What has he done to my little Roger?'

Whereupon her little Roger opened his left eye and twitched at her. It produced the loudest scream of the night. And only then did it dawn on them that they'd been had.

Nobody spoke to either Roger or me for the rest of the tour. But it was worth it.

14 The Jobsworth

A Jobsworth is an official – usually in uniform and almost certainly wearing a cap (the cap being a symbol of authority). He's also unco-operative. Despite repeated requests for assistance, despite reason, threats or bribes, he'll always intone: 'Sorry, mate, it's more than me jobsworth.'

Of course he's not really sorry at all. He enjoys untold power in the authority vested in him and is determined to elevate himself, in his own eyes, as far as the cap will allow.

There are two ways of dealing with a Jobsworth: either walk away in search of a larger cap or play him at his own game – a dangerous gambit but sometimes effective. You have to steel yourself to be equally belligerent and be ready to launch yourself confidently on the attack. If you pull it off, nine times out of ten the Jobsworth will transfer his bullying attitude to his nearest bare-headed minion, leaving you to look on and admire his position of power. When that happens you've cracked it; he can't do enough for you.

Such was the case at a gig in the Midlands once. I'd stopped working under contract to Larry by then: we'd come to an arrangement whereby I was free to work under different management provided I still did his two yearly shows – at a reduced rate, of course. Gigs could bring in as much as £300 a night, which was good money in those days for an hour or a couple of half-hour spots at a ballroom. Work hard and you could make yourself some proper money. Which is why me and me Bruvvers were travelling in a rusty Dormobile looking for a Victorian town hall at three o'clock one Sunday afternoon after driving all night from Aberdeen – this Midlands part of the tour being the result of my new manager's twisted geographical sense of humour.

Eventually we found it. Pulling up sharply, and taking care that the vicious sliding door peculiar to this refrigerated coffin on wheels didn't take the top off an elbow again, we all staggered out on to the pavement, trailing behind us a deluge of empty beer bottles, crisp packets and orange peel. The Bass Player, his bum numb from sitting on the engine cover (the best seat in the house), limped out and began to unload the gear while I went in search of life.

The Town Hall was one of those buildings standing like an island in its own block. I began walking round it, tapping gently on the doors, it being Sunday. By the fourth lap I was hammering at them with a microphone stand. Not a bloody soul was to be seen.

''Sa winda up there, mate,' said the Drummer, flicking his nose in the direction of a small panel of grime some ten feet from the footpath.

'Give us a back then,' I said and climbed up on his shoulders. One thing about drummers: they're pretty anthropoid. The window needed a bit of a spit and a rub of the sleeve, but soon enough I'd cleared a patch to peer through. There, sitting in an old horsehair armchair, warming his feet in front of an iron stove, was a man. I tapped on the window. He didn't move. Asleep. I tapped again, harder, and whistled. Still no response. The Drummer's back gave way and I fell to the ground. It started to rain. This was getting ridiculous.

'P'raps he's dead,' said the Bass Player reverently.

'P'raps he's deaf,' shouted the Drummer, being deaf himself.

'He's asleep on the job,' I said, sitting on the pavement.

'Why doncha stand on the van?' asked the Groupie.

'Who asked you?' we all said. But it was a good idea. I backed the van up against the wall and we all stood on the roof, shouting and gesticulating through the window. Slowly his head turned, he looked straight at us . . . and then he turned back to the stove.

It dawned on us. We were being ignored.

'Break the bloody winda,' screamed the Drummer.

'Don't be daft,' said the Bass Player. 'It ain't a notel room.'

Short of smashing the window we did everything we could to attract his attention. For ten minutes we hurled threats and abuse at him. Finally, just as the Drummer's thoughts were getting exciting, he stirred, reached for his cap and disappeared through a door on the far side of his cubby hole.

Another fifteen minutes passed. We'd had enough. We were loading our now-sodden equipment back into the van when a nearby door opened and a face appeared.

'What the bleedin' 'ell do you lot want?'

Section 25, sub-section B of the Union of Council Caretakers' rule book. Good public relations.

'We're the group,' I said, all polite. Musicians' rule book. Get your gear inside before you kick the bastard's head in.

'I thought you were the group. Well, you're not 'ere till eight o'clock.'

Funny, I thought. We're here now.

'Just a mo', mate,' I yelled as he was moving his head behind the door. 'We've got to set up our gear and 'ave something to eat before the show.'

'You'll be lucky. Nuffink open round 'ere – least of all this building.'

There he goes again. 'You're 'ere,' we all said.

'Yes, but I'm the official custodian of these premises. And it's more than my jobsworth to let anyone in.'

I glared at him. He glared at me. We glared at each other for a few minutes more while out of the corner of one eye I could see the lads pooling their money to see if we had enough for the petrol back to London. That was serious. It was all right for them, they were getting paid weekly. But for me it was no play, no pay. This called for desperate measures. Back I went to the van, grabbed an old road tax form – suitably official-looking – from behind the front seat and stomped back to the Jobsworth, waving it in his face.

'See this,' I snarled. 'D'you know what it is? It's a contract. That's right, a contract. An' it says 'ere that we'll be met at (I thought quickly) three o'clock by an official of the Council who will look after us and see that we have everything we need. It's signed' (I looked at the bottom of the form) 'by the mayor.' I gave this a chance to sink in. 'As you're the only one here, you must be his official representative.'

The Jobsworth beamed at this new-found status. I'd got the bastard.

After that it was easy. He made us tea, which we had in the mayor's chambers. After all, he was his official representative – and he had all the keys. As we soon found out when he insisted on giving us a guided tour of the Town Hall. Round and round we went, and as time passed by so did our chances of a decent nosh before the show. We still had to set up our gear.

Finally, after 'This is the mayor's parlour' and 'This is where the mayor receives his council', we came upon two massive mahogany doors. At last, I thought. The ballroom.

'And this,' he said, throwing open the huge portals and flinging his arms wide. 'This' (his voice assumed the ambience of the great hall) 'is where the mayor holds his balls and dances.'

It almost made the day worthwhile.

15 Nuggy McGrath

The first time I toured Ireland produced some of the funniest experiences of my life. Not at the time, mind you. According to the contract, we were booked to perform at all the top ballrooms in the Republic. In truth it was a different story. A different story every night, come to think of it.

'Sure 'n' all that's a lovely piece of paper with all those fine words on it.'

It began the evening Nuggy McGrath picked us up at the airport. Nuggy was the tour organizer.

'I'll be handlin' all yer travel arrangements personally meself, lads.'

Which meant he drove the bus. Which proved to be the inevitable Dormobile. In we piled, luggage and all, and trundled off to an unknown destination – The Hotel. We trundled for miles.

'How far now, Nuggy?' we kept asking. 'How bloody far?'

'Sure 'n' it's not far now,' Nuggy replied with the catchphrase for which he was to become famous. He turned to beam at us all and the Dormobile careered from one side of the road to the other before resuming its rightful place in the middle. As far as miles and Nuggy were concerned, to get anywhere near the truth you had to divide by two, multiply by four and take away the number you first thought of. It was the same with time.

It goes without saying that Nuggy McGrath was King of the Blarney. He'd kissed the stone so many times that the priest had stopped hearing his confession. It's because of Nuggy that Bert Weedon, to this day, still believes in The Little People. What he doesn't know is that Nuggy set him up. Nuggy, you see, had this friend who was a midget, and this midget had a leprechaun's outfit, a little green suit with a green bowler hat, funny shoes with brass buckles, and an enormous shillelagh.

The trick was that Nuggy would wind up all the visiting personalities by telling them stories about 'The Wee Folk'. Then, usually on the way home from a gig, Nuggy would flash his headlights at a prearranged spot and out into the road would run the little fellow. He had it down to a fine art, staying in the headlights just long enough without overdoing it. So convinced was Bert that if you mention The Little People to him now he simply gives a knowing wink.

Meanwhile we're still trundling along in the Dormobile and the Drummer's asking Nuggy what the chances are of something to eat when we get there.

'Sure 'n' aren't de restaurants open 365 hours a day in Ireland. When we get dere, lads, y' can take yer pick.'

And shovel it down.

'When are we gonna get there then, Nuggy?'

All together now.

'SURE 'N' IT'S NOT FAR NOW!'

We'd rumbled Nuggy in the first few hours. Or so we thought. When we arrived at our destination, the place where the hotel was supposed to be, the whole town was in darkness. The only light I could see came from a telephone box. It hadn't occurred to anyone to vandalize it yet.

'Where's all the night life then, Nuggy?' asked the Bass Player from where he was sitting on the engine cover.

'Holy Mary, mother of God,' said Nuggy. 'Didn't I just forget now. It's de one day o' de year dat everyting closes early.'

'What about the hotel?' I asked.

'Sure, y'll be all right dere now. I've had a word wid dem 'n' dey're laying on a five-course meal for you lads.'

We looked at each other. We looked at Nuggy. His face was a picture of innocent benevolence. Or was it benevolent innocence? There was no way of knowing with Nuggy.

SCREECH!

We all shot forward. Nuggy was standing on the brakes and we were sliding and wobbling to a halt outside a ramshackle three-storey building.

'Here we are, lads. De hotel. 'N' if y' don't mind I'll just be dropping yez here and be on me way. I've a lot to sort out before I picks yez up in de morning.'

We tumbled out of the van, cases in hand, and stood looking at our home for the night. It was bloody awful.

'All right for y', lads?' enquired Nuggy as, without waiting for a reply, he let out the clutch and lurched away, yelling 'I'll be round in de morning.'

'Oi, Nuggy, just a minute,' I shouted after him, 'the office said we'd be staying at the Sheraton.'

'Dat's right,' came his diminishing reply. 'Mrs Sheraton.'

Mrs Sheraton had obviously gone to bed. It was, after all, three o'clock in the morning. We were still banging on the door at a quarter to four.

'There's nobody here,' said the Bass Player.

''Ang on a minute,' said the Drummer. 'I 'eard summink.'

From somewhere at the back of the house a door slammed: almost simultaneously the front door opened and a bloke was standing on the step wearing a pair of striped pyjamas buttoned right up to the neck. On his feet were a pair of heavy hobnailed boots, fully laced. I peered closer. Beneath the pyjamas he was fully dressed.

'Sure 'n' it's a cold night to be sure,' he said by way of explanation, catching me looking at him. ''N' what can I be doin' for yez at this very early hour?'

'He's Joe Brown and we're His Bruvvers,' said the Bass Player.

'Sure now, 'n' very proud of yez yer mother must be.'

'No, we're a band. Joe Brown and His Bruvvers. That's our name. We thought you'd be expecting us.'

'With a five-course dinner,' said the Drummer.

'Didn't Nuggy McGrath tell you we were coming?' I asked.

'Oh, Nuggy!' The farthing had dropped. 'No, no, he didn't. But come in all de same.' He stood back to let us pass. 'Y' see, I tought yez maight be someone else,' he said, tapping his nose and winking.

'Sinus trouble,' said the Rhythm Guitarist, and we trouped down the corridor into the kitchen. Somewhere in the yard outside someone was trying to start a car.

'Sit yerselves down, lads,' said our host in a hurry. 'I won't be long.'

Out he rushed through the back door.

'It's all right, lads!' we heard him yell. 'It's some fella wid his relations.'

Back he came, unbuttoning his pyjamas.

'D'yer know, wid all dat bangin' 'n' all, I tought yez maight be de polis. Now sit yerselves down now and tell me all about yerselves.'

I was starting to tell him that we were over to do a tour of the top ballrooms in the south of Ireland when the back door opened again and these five big burly blokes came marching through the kitchen, weighed down by a variety of suspicious-looking duffel bags that clanked ominously. Without a word they filed past us and disappeared through a door which looked as if it led to a cellar.

I'll kill that bugger, McGrath, I thought. I'll give him to the Drummer for breakfast. What the hell does he think he's playing at?

The five-course meal turned out to be a round of cheese and onion sandwiches each and two pints of Guinness between the four of us. We spent the night huddled together in one freezing-cold room on straw mattresses.

About ten o'clock the next morning Nuggy turned up wearing a huge grin that almost split his face in two.

'Top o' de morning, lads. I trust y' all slept well.'

Bloody cheek.

The Drummer took a step forward and Nuggy's face came together in a second. The Bass Player kicked shut the kitchen door.

'Now look, Nuggy,' I said. 'We came here to work, but there's no way we're even going to unpack our gear until we get a few things straightened out. For a start, we can't stay here.'

Nuggy raised his finger to his lips. I lowered my voice.

'It's not that the Sheratons aren't nice people.'

'It's just that he sleeps with his boots on,' said the Bass Player.

'It's just that we can't sleep with all that noise coming up from the cellar. I don't know what they're doing down there, and to be honest, Nuggy, I don't want to know. Just get us out of here for a start and then we'll talk.'

'Sure, sure, lads,' said Nuggy, all expansive. 'Would I expect yez to stay in a place like dis wid all dat clanging goin' on? It's de wheelchairs.'

'Wheelchairs!' I exclaimed. 'What wheelchairs?'

'Dey makes 'em in de cellar, y'know. For de old people's homes.' He put his fingers to his lips once more. 'But I wouldn't mention it to anyone. In Ireland y' need a licence for dat sort o' ting, 'n' sure aren't dey just tryin' to do de old folks a good turn.'

We looked at him in utter amazement. Where did he get them from?

'Right, Nuggy,' I said. 'That's it. We're off.'

And as one we picked up our bags and marched into the street.

'Now don't be hasty, lads,' cried Nuggy, chasing after us. 'Sure 'n' wasn't I only joking. Just get in de car now and we'll find yez a nice hotel.'

Car! We looked around and there, standing at the curb, was a large, black Humber Snipe. Old, admittedly, but a Humber Snipe all the same. Things were looking up. We got in the car, Nuggy drove off, nobody said a word. I don't think anyone could take any more bullshit. A few miles down the road we came to a small guesthouse. Simple but nice. Mind you, anything would have looked better than the bloody Sheraton.

'Who owns this place then, Nuggy?' said the Drummer. 'Mrs Hilton?'

'Har har har,' laughed Nuggy sourly. I think he was getting the message.

We went into the guesthouse and made sure that Nuggy stayed around until we were happy. We had a gig that night and wanted to be certain we had somewhere to stay afterwards. It seemed all right.

'Right den, lads,' Nuggy said. 'I better leave yez now. I've got t' pick up de bus and collect yer instruments from de airport. I'll be back wid de car about six o'clock to take yez to de first gig.'

There was something in the way he said 'first gig' that made me feel uneasy – but it was too late to say anything. Nuggy was proving himself to be the master of the fast getaway. It would have to wait. And I mean wait. That evening he turned up at a quarter to seven.

'I thought you said you'd be here at six,' I told him. 'You're three-quarters of an hour late.'

'Sure 'n' don't y' be worrying yerselves. This is Ireland. We do tings different over here. Y' die young if y' rush around.'

'That's all very well, but what time are we due on? And how far is it?'

Nuggy looked pensive.

'In answer to yer first question' – he thought hard – 'not too late. In answer to yer second question' – he thought harder – 'not too far.'

I wasn't satisfied.

'That's not good enough, Nuggy. What time and how far?'

He thought a while, then said very quickly: 'Seven o'clock 'n' forty miles.' He took a breath. 'Give or take a few yards.'

'What do you mean a few yards?' I motioned the Drummer forward.

'Ah, well, all right den, fifty miles – or so.'

This was getting stupid. I was getting angry.

'Nuggy, it's five to seven now. How are we going to do fifty miles, or so, in five minutes?'

'Dat car,' he waved his arm proudly towards the old car. 'Dat automobile is the fastest car in da whole of Ireland. 'N' sure now, didn't da Michael Murphy himself use it to make his getaway from da polis after dat business at da munitions factory. So come on, lads, jump in and I'll have yez dere before y' can say Killarney.'

We grabbed our stuff, jumped aboard and shot off down the road at a steady twenty miles an hour. Two hours later we were still travelling.

'Bloody hell, Nuggy,' moaned the Drummer, 'how much further?'

He shouldn't have asked.

'Sure 'n' it's not far now.'

Everybody groaned.

We heard the place before we saw it. The sounds of fighting and breaking glass. The old car turned a final corner and there we were: outside an old barn. Bedlam issued from its doors.

'Nuggy,' I asked, 'is this it?'

'Sure 'n' I tink it might be.'

'But we're supposed to be playing at all the top ballrooms in the south of Ireland.'

'So you are. So you are. 'Tis just dat yer a few minutes late now and de natives is getting restless wid de waitin' fer yez.'

To prove his point, just then a big bloke crashed through one of the front windows, landing on his back with a sickening thud.

'Bejesus, I'll get yer fer dat, Mary Donovan!' He staggered to his feet and stumbled back inside.

That's great, I thought. MARY Donovan.

Nuggy drove the car along a track beside the hall to the back, where a priest was pacing up and down reading his breviary.

'Hello dere, Fadder,' hailed Nuggy. 'Dey're here.'

'Holy Mary,' exclaimed the priest, snapping the book shut. 'Tank God y've come at last. Dey're going berserk in dere.'

'Sorry dey're late, Fadder. We stopped to give a poor soul a lift to de hospital. I tink her mother must've been dying and . . .'

'Yes yes yes,' interrupted the priest, not believing a word of it. 'Well, yer here now, tanks be to God. Get dem on de stage quick now before dey smashes up de place.'

We were bundled unceremoniously through the back door and straight on to the stage where all the guitars and the drum kit were set up waiting for us. At least Nuggy had got that right. As soon as the audience saw us they quietened down immediately: usually we had the opposite effect. It was great. They were a smashing audience (if you see what I mean): genuinely pleased to see us. And before long we were rocking away, having a grand time. We did something like five encores and came off the stage feeling absolutely knackered. The priest was over the moon.

'Sure, we haven't had a night like dis since Sean Donaghue's wake.' He took hold of Nuggy's arm. 'Now you 'n' the lads come with me, Nuggy, and we'll show dem a little Irish hospitality.'

Nuggy shook his head.

'I'm sorry, Fadder, but de lads is all tired out to deir bones 'n' I've said I'll take dem back to deir hotel.'

'Hang on, Nuggy,' I said. 'Just a minute. Me and the boys are all right. We wouldn't mind a pint or two.'

'Besides,' said the Drummer, 'you're driving.'

'Now, now, lads. We've got sixty miles to go and yez got yer strength t' keep up.'

'Sixty miles now, is it?'

'Give or take a few yards,' said Nuggy, pushing us towards the car. As soon as we were in, Nuggy was off like a bat out of hell, screaming round the corners and touching sixty through all the small villages.

'For Christ's sake slow down,' yelled the Drummer. 'What's the hurry?'

He soon got his answer. Nuggy swung the Humber into the car park of a large pub, seething with people.

'I tought I'd stop 'n' treat yez t' dat pint y' was on about.'

I didn't say anything but I smelt a rat. And I was right. As soon as we were through the door we were pushed straight on stage again. There wasn't a thing we could do about it. Somebody else's guitars were thrust in our hands and the Drummer was pushed behind the worst kit I've ever seen – or heard, come to that. It was diabolical.

By the time we finally got off the stage we were all speechless with anger. Even Nuggy realized he'd gone too far this time, and as soon as I got him on his own I went crazy.

'You bastard!' I screamed. 'You lying greedy cheating bastard! You've known about this all along, haven't you? You knew we were supposed to do only one show a night and you planned this, didn't you? It was all worked out before we left the hotel, wasn't it? Well, that's it. We're finished. We've had enough. We're off back to England in the morning.'

He didn't say a word. Just got the car and drove us to the guesthouse. There was silence all the way. But next morning, bright as a lark, he was back there while we were still having breakfast.

'Top o' da morning, lads. I trust yez slept well.'

We couldn't help laughing. The cheek of the bloke. The Drummer poured him a cup of tea.

'Well, now, lads, have y' decided what yez want to do?'

'We know what we'd like to do to you,' said the Bass Player.

'Now listen, lads. I'm sorry I wasn't straight wid yer but y' must understand that we don't get many good shows over here, and de truth is I could've sold dis show out five times a night. De people here are just ordinary working folk and to dem it means so much. Why now, d'yer know dat some o' dem have been looking forward to dis for months. Savin' up deir hard-earned pennies,' (he removed his hat and clutched it to his chest) 'just to hear Joe Brown and His Bruvvers.

'Now at de show tonight, de show yez were *supposed* to be doin' tonight, dere's dis little lame lad called Patrick, and his poor mother Mary . . .'

'All right, Nuggy,' I interrupted. I couldn't take any more. The Bass Player's tears were making the toast soggy. 'Cut the blarney. You win. But no more bullshit, right?'

'Oh!' His face lit up. 'Oh. Right.'

Things got better after that. It turned out that Nuggy had double-booked us most nights, but at least we knew what was happening and where we were going. The blarney didn't stop altogether, but then with a bloke like Nuggy you couldn't expect the impossible. And it didn't prevent him from trying his Little People trick on us.

We were coming back from a gig – sorry, two gigs – a week later when he started.

'Have y' ever heard of leprechauns?' he asked.

'Do you have to have an injection for it?' asked the Bass Player.

'No, no, ye' don't understand. Leprechauns.' He lowered his voice. 'Leprechauns is de little people.'

'What, like Charlie Drake?' said the Drummer and we all laughed.

'Sure 'n' it's no laughing matter now. Why, only de udder day dey caught a little fella no bigger dan yer tumb. Dey put him in a bottle and de whole of Dublin saw him.'

'Did you see him, Nuggy?' I asked.

'Well, no, not exactly, but I had it on good autority from Mad Murphy.'

We laughed our heads off but Nuggy couldn't see the joke.

'Listen,' he said, all serious, 'don't tink dat I never seed one. Dere's many a night I've been drivin' along a quiet road 'n' heard dem singin' in de fields.'

He jammed on the brakes, brought the car to a halt and wound down his window.

'Now yez just listen,' he said.

'Come on, Nuggy,' groaned the Drummer. 'Let's go 'ome.'

'No, no. Just listen now.'

We sat there for ten minutes or so in utter silence and pitch darkness. Not a sound. Not even the swish of a shillelagh.

'Come on, Nuggy,' I told him, having had enough of the nonsense, 'we're tired and we're hungry. Let's get back.'

'Yeah, come on, man,' said the Bass Player. 'This is all a load of rubbish.'

'Rubbish!' said Nuggy, getting unusually annoyed. 'Rubbish! Now yez never should have said dat. If dey hears yer say dat y'll bring down de wrath o' de king of de fairies hisself and we'll all be turned to stone.'

He put his hand to his ear.

'Dere!' he whispered fiercely. 'Did yer hear it?'

We strained our ears and the Drummer picked his nose. Not a bloody thing.

'Well I heard it,' argued Nuggy angrily, ''N' I'm not moving from dis place until y' say y' can hear dem too.'

He yanked on the handbrake to emphasize his point.

We waited.

'I heard it!' yelled the Bass Player. 'Now let's go home.'

'What about you?' Nuggy asked the Drummer.

'No!' he growled defiantly.

The Bass Player dug an elbow in the Drummer's ribs.

'Yes!'

Another dig.

'Definitely.'

'OK, Nuggy,' I said. 'We've all heard them. Now can we go home, please?'

'T' be sure. But first we all have to tell dem goodnight.'

So there we were, sitting in the pitch dark, shouting across the fields:

'GOODNIGHT, FAIRIES, GOODNIGHT!'

Thank the fairies nobody heard us.

Most of the halls we played in on that tour belonged to the Catholic church, which meant the gigs were usually run by the local priest. And in that part of Ireland the priest's power was paramount. Generally speaking he was respected: sometimes loved, sometimes feared. Some were kind; some ruled the roost – if you'll excuse the expression – with a rod of iron. Or in the case of the last dance we played, the leg of a chair.

It came about like this.

Nuggy had picked us up on the afternoon of our last day in Ireland. Another two-gig jig: one at six, the other at eight. True, we were a bit late getting on the road but we thought we had plenty of time. Only we hadn't bargained on the hay wagon. We were stuck behind this thing for fifteen miles – give or take a yard or so – doing five miles an hour down these winding country roads. Even Nuggy was getting rattled. He put his hand on the horn and tried to pass. No way. So it went on, until eventually the farmer stopped the wagon and came ambling back towards the car. The harder he looked at it the more his face lit up like a Christmas tree.

'Well, well, now, well, well. T' be sure, well, well. If it isn't me very own long lost cousin, Nuggy McGrath.'

'Holy Jesus,' Nuggy muttered, pulling his hat down over his face and sliding down in his seat.

The farmer stomped round the car with a meaningful look, and as he passed the driver's door he brought a huge brown fist crashing down on the roof. The car reverberated like an empty dustbin and we all had to hold our noses and blow to clear our ears.

'Come on out, Nuggy. I knows yer dere. I can recognize me own car when I sees it.'

My stomach turned. This was it. We had trouble. Nuggy tried to bluff his way out of it from where he was, low down in his seat. He pretended he hadn't heard. He reached down to the clutch pedal and started to tug at it violently.

'Sure 'n' all, lads, 'n' won't we soon have it fixed. 'N' won't me dear cousin Seamus be pleased at all de trouble we've gone to t' put it right again.' He looked up as the door was yanked open. 'Well, well, hello dere, Seamus. 'N' wasn't I just talking to de lads about y' now.' He grinned weakly.

Dear cousin Seamus wasn't having any of it.

'Out,' he bellowed.

Nuggy got out. The Drummer, Bass Player and Rhythm Guitarist huddled together in the back for protection. Snatches of the conversation drifted through the open door.

Seamus: 'Y' said yez wanted it for de funeral.'

Nuggy: ''N' sure wasn't de corpse's wife grateful.'

Seamus: 'But dat was last Tursday fortnight and today's Saturday.'

Nuggy: 'Sure 'n' isn't she still grateful.'

Seamus: 'Nuggy McGrath, you're a scheming lying toad.'

Nuggy: 'Tank you, Seamus, tank you.'

So it went on. Twenty minutes passed. Eventually money changed hands and a rueful Nuggy made his way back to the car. True to form, though, he soon brightened up.

'Dat was me dear cousin Seamus whom I haven't seen for so long I felt it me duty to stop 'n' pass de time o' day with him.'

'Talking of time, Nuggy,' I said, 'hadn't we better get a move on? We're supposed to be at the gig at six, and it's a quarter to seven now.'

'Is dat right?' said Nuggy. ''N' sure doesn't time fly when y're enjoyin' yerself. We'll just wait till Cousin Seamus pulls the wagon up on the bank so we can get past.'

Sure enough the wagon was lurching forwards. But as it began to turn to negotiate the steep bank at the side of the road . . . I don't need to tell you what happened. Half an hour later we were all still struggling to load three tons of hay bales back on the wagon. What's more, dear Cousin Seamus refused to help. I'm sure he did it on purpose.

By now we were very late, yet when eventually we did get to the church hall, at about ten past eight, they were surprisingly mild about our late arrival.

'I heard what a good show you've got for us,' the priest told Nuggy when he tried to apologize. 'A little patience is good for the soul. It'll do them good to wait for a while.'

On we went – to another great reception. Everything was going just as it should until, out of the corner of my eye, I caught sight of Nuggy frantically drawing his finger across his throat. He was mouthing something that looked like 'Cut! Cut!' What was he swearing at me for?

Next solo I hopped over to where he was standing.

'What's the matter, Nuggy?'

'One more song!' he screamed. 'One more and get OFF!'

We finished the number and I went across to talk to Nuggy in the wings. He was trying to compose himself.

'Ah, Joe,' he began and I knew we had a problem. 'Remember I told yez we had two shows tonight.'

'That's right,' I said. 'One at six and one at eight.'

'One at six 'n' one at eight. Yes. Dat's right. Well, now, I don't know how t' tells y' this, Joe.' He swallowed hard. I knew what was coming.

'Don't tell me. We're at the wrong gig.'

He nodded. His face was as white as a sheet, nose and all. We had a steaming audience out front waiting for me to go back on – and God alone knew what was happening at the other place. It was unbelievable. Two gigs: one at six, one at eight and we do the eight o'clock gig first. No wonder they weren't worried. The priest's words came back to me. 'A little patience is good for the soul.' A *little* patience! They'll lynch us.

It seemed an age before we finished the set. Meanwhile down in the dressing-room Nuggy was going berserk.

'What're we goin' to do? What're we goin' to do?'

'Phone them.'

'I have phoned dem. I've phoned dem tree times but it's no good. Dey're not on de phone.'

'Nuggy,' I said, grabbing him, 'don't panic. How far is it?'

'Sure 'n' it's not . . .' He gave up and his voice broke with a sob of despair. 'It's fifty bloody miles,' he cried. It was the only time I heard him swear.

'Look,' I said, 'I'll tell you what. You and I'll go in the car. The boys can stay behind, load up the gear and come on after us. At least they'll know we're coming.'

'Why don't we all go in the car?' the Bass Player suggested. 'We can use the gear there.'

'Dere isn't any udder gear dere. You're de only band.'

This was getting worse. But there was no other way out. Not bothering to change, I grabbed what gear I could and jumped in the car. Nuggy drove like a maniac. We were there in under an hour.

Never in my life did I think I'd see a dance hall like the one we played the first night. But that had nothing on this. A wooden building with a corrugated iron roof, it was probably built to accommodate three hundred people. Jammed inside right now there must have been over six hundred people, all shoulder to shoulder, trying to hit each other across the head of the person between them. There were empty Guinness bottles flying everywhere, the noise was deafening and the priest was on stage trying to restore order.

'Calm down now! Calm down now!' he was shouting at the top of his voice as Nuggy and I slipped in through the back door. 'Dey'll be here soon.'

He was a huge man, with great hairy arms poking from an enormous black cassock. Nuggy waved to him from the side of the stage, pointing at me, and next thing I knew I was being lifted bodily on to the stage. The priest simply grabbed me by the back of my coat, held me at arm's length in one mighty paw and shook me in front of the crowd like a rag doll. I swear my feet never touched the ground.

'Look! Look!' he screamed. 'He's here! He's here!'

He let go and I fell unceremoniously on to the stage. A buzz went round the hall as everybody looked at me. A deathly hush fell. A sudden ceasefire had been declared. I scrambled to my feet to face the hostile crowd. I was terrified. When I opened my mouth to apologize, nothing came out. The Parnes should have seen me now.

'Just keep calm,' said the priest, coming to my rescue. 'Now den,' he addressed the congregation. 'Now den. Dat's better. A little quiet now 'n' we'll get de show started. Never, never in me born days have I seen de like of such shenanigans. As for you, Patrick O'Donoghue,' he said pointing meaningfully at a bloke standing in the front row, 'you started dis and if y' causes any more trouble it'll be me y'll be dealing with.'

'Sure 'n' it wasn't me, Fadder,' said the accused. 'It was O'Reilly over dere.'

Rumblings from O'Reilly's direction. 'Why now, dat's a dirty rotten lie' preceded a flying Guinness bottle which struck the man next to O'Donoghue on the head. He didn't even flinch.

'ENOUGH!' roared the priest. 'Dat's enough. Just be patient.' And as an afterthought, 'It's good for de soul.'

He stormed off stage, dragging me with him to a small dressing-room where we tried to work out a plan of action. Basically there was nothing we could do until the van arrived with the rest of the gear, and that could be another hour. Then we still had to set up for the show. The priest had said a few minutes. It wouldn't have been so bad if there'd been another group to keep them amused but they were just standing there, packed together like sardines, waiting. Like they'd been waiting since six o'clock. It was now twenty past eleven. We were nearly five and a half hours late. Even in Ireland that was late.

'Look, Father,' I appealed to the priest, 'can't we cancel the show?'

'Cancel it!' he cried with a shudder. 'D'y' know what would happen if we cancelled it?'

I shook my head.

'Neither do I,' he said and crossed himself. Cancelling was obviously out of the question.

Ten minutes passed and fighting was breaking out again in the hall.

'Dey're at it again,' muttered the priest. 'Follow me.'

Nuggy and I trailed behind him towards the stage, where once more he grabbed me by the coat collar and carried me in front of him to face the crowd. I thought he said we were to follow him. This was a case of follow me, I'll be right behind you.

'Now den, now den. A little quiet 'n' we'll have de show started in a couple o' minutes.' Same spiel as before. Same dressing-down for Patrick O'Donoghue, who this time stood there looking sheepish. This routine happened another three or four times before the van arrived, and as quick as we could we set up the gear. There was still some aggravation but at least they could see they were getting a show. However, when at long last we struck the first chord we knew we'd gone past the point of redemption. Ten minutes into the set there were fists, feet, curses and bottles flying about like bluebottles in a butcher's yard. The Drummer was crouched behind his kit, using his cymbals as a shield. It gave a new dimension to the phrase 'front line'. We were in it with a vengeance.

Bottles were bouncing everywhere and it's a miracle no one was seriously hurt. Suddenly I had a bright idea. Leaning across to the microphone amplifier I turned the master volume up to full. The hall was filled with a terrible screeching as the mikes fed back. Stunned silence throughout the place. I turned them down again to working level and spoke into my mike.

'Please. Please. I don't expect you to have any respect for the music we've played so far. But now we'd like to play you – a hymn.'

It worked. They all listened attentively while we played 'All Things Bright and Beautiful', the only hymn we knew even if none of them did. You could have heard a pin drop. But as soon as we'd finished, they were at it again.

'Quick,' I shouted, ' "Johnny B. Goode".'

We went steaming straight in, but by the time we got to the guitar solo they were actually fighting *on* the stage. Out came the guitar leads, over went the drum kit, down went the microphone stands.

ON CAME THE PRIEST.

A frightening sight to see. Like a mad bull. Throwing bodies aside like a combine harvester in a field full of wheat. He gained the centre of the stage, raised himself to his full height and lifted his cassock to his waist, producing as if by magic a long piece of wood. It was the leg of a chair. Everybody backed away. Everybody, that is, except Patrick O'Donoghue. He wasn't so fortunate. The priest brought the leg of the chair crashing down on the skull of the unfortunate troublemaker.

'Take dat!' said the priest, and immediately looked towards heaven, intoning 'God forgive me' and blessing himself.

I think he lost his temper then. He stood there on the stage roaring, his arms akimbo, the sleeves of the great black cassock hanging from them like the wings of an avenging angel. Suddenly, without warning, he made a perfect swallow dive into the seething mass of bodies cowering before him.

'Take dat!' I could hear as he advanced, wielding the chair leg as he went. 'Take dat!' CRACK! 'May God forgive me. Take dat!' CRACK! 'May God forgive me. Take dat!' CRACK! All the way down the hall until only the CRACK was audible, though I could still see him glancing heavenwards and blessing himself.

How we got away from there in one piece I'll never know. But I do know that it was a long long time before I played Ireland again.

16 Another Irish story

I've always had a thing about wigs. And the people who wear them. How a grown man could put his faith into anything so unreliable is something I could never understand. Granted, some are very good and not obvious. But most of them are dreadful bodge-ups that look as if they've been cut off the back of a cornflake packet at breakfast – by a five-year-old.

Nothing fascinates me more than to be sitting in a seaside restaurant when one comes bobbing in, supported by its alien host who, forgetting the wig, is wearing a look of supreme confidence. Where does it come from? And what price vanity? He stands there beaming while the waiter seats his lady. Then he sits down himself and accepts the menu. Self-assurance radiates. But watch the waiter, evilly lingering. From where he stands he can see it in all its glory. Our man turns.

'My wife will have a prawn cocktail. I'll have the brown Windsor soup. To follow, lamb chops and a sirloin steak. Oh, and the wine list, please.'

'Certainly, sir,' bows the waiter, edging backwards, unable to take his eyes off the ginger monstrosity.

'Charlie!' he shouts through the hatch. 'Wine list. Table four. The geezer wiv the rug.'

'The geezer wiv the rug' must have heard him, and yet he sits there undaunted, unembarrassed. Why, I ask myself. Why?

My local doctor approached me once. I thought he wanted me to pay his bill.

'Look, Joe, you're in show business. You couldn't recommend a good wig-maker, could you?'

'Yeah, I suppose so. Who for?'

He came closer and whispered in my ear.

'For me.'

'For you!' I laughed. 'What do you want one of those bloody things stuck on your bonce for?'

One look at his face and I could've bitten my tongue off. He was crestfallen.

'Well, you know, I just sort of thought . . .' His voice trailed off into silence and I sloped off into the distance. Next time I saw him it was painfully obvious he had taken my criticism to heart. What little hair he still had was sprouting in well-cultivated but very isolated clumps which he had let grow as long as possible. These strands were then combed in a criss-cross fashion at different angles across the top of his head so that it resembled one of those raffia table mats. A rug on his jug couldn't have looked worse.

The funniest case I ever knew was Eric from Liverpool. He was a mate of Neil, who was married to my sister-in-law and, despite this or perhaps because of it, had a great sense of humour. In Liverpool you need one.

When it comes to wigs, Neil cannot be relied on to keep a straight face: especially when it's Eric's wig. We'd be sitting in the kitchen – Neil and Mary, my wife Vicki and me and Rob, my father-in-law – when the cry would go up from Neil.

'Quick, here's Eric!'

Everyone would dash to the front window to watch as Eric, sitting outside in his Cortina, made last-minute adjustments to his Irish before he came in. The performance could take as long as ten minutes. Then he'd walk through the door, look you straight in the eye and ask 'How is it?'

'How's what, Eric?' someone would ask, whereupon, keeping his head perfectly still, he'd flick both eyes ceilingwards before returning to stare piercingly at you.

'You know,' he'd say. 'You know.'

And then the ritual would start.

Neil: 'Can't see the join, pal.'

Me: 'Looks like you were born with it.'

Vicki: 'It's like real hair.'

Neil: 'Wish I had one.'

Rob: 'Can you get 'em in any colour?'

Mary: 'How much are they?'

Eric would beam happily.

(*Long embarrassing silence.*)
Neil: 'It's bloody horrible.'
All: Hysterical laughter.
Exit Eric, weeping.

Poor Eric. So conscious was he of his baldness that he would go to the most outrageous lengths to disguise it. His weekly swim was a fine example. Every Friday night he'd finish work about six and go to the swimming-baths to freshen up in preparation for his night job as compere at the Wookey Hollow Club – no mean task. Off would come his grey suit, blue shirt, maroon tie and hush puppies: on would go his bathing trunks. Then, looking round to make sure no one was watching, he'd whip off the wig and quickly don a yellow bathing cap with little rubber flowers on it. Should anyone come in unexpectedly before he'd achieved this sleight of hand, he'd start running on the spot, his bare feet slapping on the tiled floor and the old Irish bobbing up and down like a dead rat on a blacksmith's bellows, puffing away and saying things like 'Hey man, it's cold tonight', or 'Whoo, hey baby'. Then, as soon as the interloper had departed, it was off with the wig and on with the bathing cap.

It was a routine that went smoothly until one particular Friday evening when he came out of the pool, dripping water and hopping into the changing-room, trying to untie the string round his ankle on which was his locker key. But it didn't matter. Someone had broken into his locker. His clothes were still there – the thief had good taste – but nicked were his wallet, his car keys – and his wig! At first Eric was frantic. Then hysterical. But he got out of it quite nicely, considering. He simply borrowed his fare and went home. A right idiot he must've looked sitting on the bus in his grey suit, blue shirt, maroon tie, hush puppies – and bright yellow bathing cap with little rubber flowers on it.

The trouble is, I'm not in a strong position to take the mickey out of Eric when it comes to wigs – not when my in-laws are around anyway. If I do they murder me, and all because I married their Vicki.

It all began during a summer season I was doing on the Britannia Pier in Yarmouth, in the days when the hardest part of the job was getting through the hordes of fans who waited outside for you after the show, especially as it finished at ten and the pubs closed at ten-thirty. It being a pier there were only two ways off: either you jumped and swam for it, or you made your way to the end of the planking to be met with delighted shrieks from the girls and more ominous sounds from their boyfriends. I soon realized that if I was going to get a drink after the show, I needed a disguise.

I bought myself a reasonable Irish and a pair of horn-rimmed glasses, and in this get-up I found I could go anywhere without being recognized. Actually the things I learnt about myself came as quite a revelation. It's surprising what people say about you when they don't know you're there.

'Joe Brown? He's a pouf, ain't he?' says the bloke next to me at the bar to the bloke standing on the other side of me.

'Nah, it's that uvver geezer, innit. What's 'is name? You know. Tommy Faith.'

'I sold 'im 'is first guitar,' says another.

'My sister used to go to school with him,' chips in another.

'Who? Joe Brown?'

'No. Tommy Faith.'

'Well, is 'e or ain't 'e?'
'What?'
'A pouf.'
'If you ask me they're all bleedin' poufs.'
'Could never play the bloody thing of course.'
'Cushy job 'e's got. Wonder what 'e really does for a living?'
All good stuff and a lot more entertaining than the show.

So by the time it came to marrying Vicki I had quite a lot of faith in this disguise. Which is more than my manager had in public opinion. He reckoned that marriage would ruin my pop star image, because at that time it was strictly taboo for a pop star to get married. Let the girls keep wishing. And hoping, and praying and hoping. The thing was, I wasn't getting any younger. Nor was Vicki and she was older than me. We'd been courting for more than four years, ever since we met on *Boy Meets Girls*. Vicki was singing with the Vernons Girls. I'd asked one of the other Vernons Girls out for a date (there were pools of them, all with perms), but when I met Vicki I asked her to join us on a double date and got the Guitar Player to take care of the first Vernons Girl. We went to see the Crazy Gang at the Victoria Palace – only it was booked up and we had to sit through *The Sound of Music* instead. Now

The Vernons Girls with one of their chaperones. Vicki is on the far right.

we'd decided the time had come to make an honest woman of Vicki. (Some hope!) But my manager, George Cooper, didn't agree with my matrimonial ambitions.

'Look what happened to Marty Wilde,' he kept saying.

'But he had flat feet before he got married,' I'd tell him. It made no difference. He was adamant. We argued about it for months. Finally it came to a head and I told him what was really on my mind.

'Look, George, I'm getting married whether you like it or not. People are beginning to say I'm a pouf.'

'What makes you think that?'

'I was in this pub in Yarmouth with me wig on and I heard this bloke tell his mate. What's more, George, he sold me my first guitar.'

'That's it,' he interrupted, failing to see the funny side of it. 'You could get married in the wig.'

'You're joking. Vicki would never wear it.'

'*She* won't have to. You will.'

I thought about it – for all of half a second.

'It won't work, George. She'll go spare.'

'She won't know about it,' repeated George. 'I'm not saying you should actually *get married* in it. Once you're inside the church you can whip it off and Bob's your uncle.'

So that was how, on 10 December, 1963, I was sitting in a car outside The Church of Christ in Thirlmere Road, Liverpool, rearranging my Irish just like Eric. Everything was set. George had taken care of the security, even down to getting a friend of his, a professional photographer, to do the photos; and Vicki's dad had pulled in some of his mates from the Royal Corps of Commissionaires to act as ushers and make sure that no one was there who shouldn't be there or took photos who shouldn't be taking photos. I slipped on the sunglasses and slipped out of the car. There were a few people around, as there always are for weddings and funerals, but none of them recognized me. I was just some four-eyed git with a dark brown barnet going into church to surrender his freedom and his manhood. I'd even darkened my eyebrows to make the disguise authentic. And that was my undoing.

Everyone, except Vicki and her dad, was already inside the church when I made my appearance, and just as I was lifting my hand to remove the wig, they all turned to look at me. My hand stopped by my jaw and froze. For some reason the thought went racing through my head that I was going to look a right fool getting married with blond hair and black eyebrows. So I scratched the side of my face, as if I had an itch, and decided to brave it out in the wig. It was a bad move.

'Sod you,' I thought, hearing someone titter as I walked down the aisle. But by the time I took my place at the front of the church I was getting the horrors. It wasn't the congregation that worried me. By now everybody in the church had got the message about what was happening. But it was Vicki. How would she react? I was soon going to find out.

The organ was playing and I could feel the chill of the breath of doom while she was still halfway down the aisle – presumably the point where she caught sight of the back of my head. It got worse when the minister, a Mr Fisher, arrived on the scene. He looked at Vick and smiled: looked at me and frowned. He quite obviously didn't recognize the bridegroom at all and began shuffling round in embarrassment, wondering what to say. Me? I was sweating with panic. Then he saw the light, and gave the assembled congregation a huge stage wink as if to say, 'We've got a prize one here.'

'Right,' he said, 'let's get on with it.'

Tentatively I reached out for Vicki's hand. It was like holding a wet haddock. I gave it a squeeze. Nothing. Not even a scale. Mr Fisher began his 'Dearly beloved' bit, but all I remember about the ceremony is thinking, What's she going to say when he gets to the bit about 'Do you take this man etcetera'. Finally we came to it.

'And will you, Victoria Haseman, take this man, Joseph Brown, to be your wedded husband, to live together after God's ordinance in the holy state of matrimony? Will you obey him, and serve him, love, honour, and keep him in sickness and in health; and, forsaking all other, keep thee only unto him, so long as you both shall live?'

Not a word. One long pause. Mr Fisher coughed and went through it all again.

'Will you, Victoria Haseman, take this man, Joseph Brown, to be your wedded husband, to live together after God's ordinance in the holy state of matrimony? Will you obey him, and serve him, love, honour and keep him, in sickness and in health; and, forsaking all other, keep thee only unto him so long as you both shall live?'

Another long pause. Then the magic words:

'I suppose so.'

Her family were having silent hysterics. Neil had almost bitten through the fist he'd stuffed in his mouth. They've never let me forget it, either. To be honest, I can't say I blame them.

Finally the ceremony was over. Not a very pleasant experience, though to be fair to Mr Fisher he managed to conduct it with a certain amount of humorous dignity. And by the time it was all signed and

From the left: Vicki's father, me, Vicki, my mum and my brother Pete, after our wedding in 1963. I'd got rid of the wig by now!

sealed, I was probably the only one who hadn't enjoyed the performance. Then, to cap it all, in the ensuing rush to get back to the house for the obligatory booze-up, Vicki's dad got left behind and had to get the bus home.

Whether George was right about marriage destroying my image I'll never be sure. But this I do know. The press did get wind of the fact, and although they hadn't any proof, they made our lives a misery for months afterwards, resorting to all sorts of tricks to discover the truth. They telephoned Mum once, saying they were the jewellers who were altering Vicki's wedding ring and did she know where they should send the bill? What she replied is unprintable except in asterisks and exclamation marks. Then one night, about six months later, there was a knock on the door and standing there were three reporters, two of them soaked to the skin. They looked as if they'd been outside, watching the house, ever since it had started raining three or four days earlier. They had!

'It's all up, Joe,' said the third reporter, who had just arrived, waving a soggy piece of paper at me. 'The game's up, mate. We've got a copy of your marriage licence.'

They had too. Looking at them standing there, wetter than water rats, I didn't have the heart to deny it. Instead I invited them in and gave them all a drink. A few drinks in fact, and that was the end of the matter. Well done, lads!

17 Stage managed

It must have been another summer season in Yarmouth that I played the Windmill Theatre for Jack Jay. Don't ask me when it was, but Billy Fury, Rolf Harris, Mark Wynter and The Tornados were on the bill, I remember that. It was a lovely little theatre, the Windmill. The only thing wrong with it was the stage manager. He was Spanish and a right git. As they say on the Costa del Yarmouth. We nicknamed him The Fly.

I can't think why we didn't like him, except that he was a poser, dashing about in a foul, greasy evening suit and always chatting up the chorus line. If ever he had some success, and even a chorus girl has to eat some time, he'd drag her off in this car he'd built from an Austin Seven. Thin little wheels it had, and him being tall he looked a proper twit in it. On the other hand it did pull the birds. 'Come for a ride in my car?' he'd suggest, and next thing you knew the miss was halfway to Diss.

He was the sort of bloke you couldn't help pulling terrible stunts on. We undid all the seams of his suit one evening: unpicked it stitch by stitch while it was hanging in the dressing-room. When he came to change into it, it simply disintegrated around him.

The worst thing we did was chain his car to Jack Jay's Bentley Continental. Stumbling across this length of anchor chain on the beach one night gave me the idea, and after that it was simply a matter of waiting for an opportunity to use it – and of keeping it hidden from the fisherman whose boat had mysteriously drifted out to sea when the tide came in. The Fly's vanity provided the opportunity, because he was so proud of this little car that he couldn't resist parking it where it would be seen by everybody – and that just happened to be right in front of Jack's Bentley.

The Windmill Theatre, Great Yarmouth.

With a little help from the Drummer, I attached one end of the chain to the Bentley's front axle and the other end to the back axle of The Fly's motor. During the show we passed the word round that it would be worth everyone's while being in the car park afterwards, so there was quite an audience when eventually he appeared from the stage door with a girl from the chorus, got in his little car, leant across and opened the door for her, and preened himself in the rear-view mirror while she got in. The Drummer and I were leaning nonchalantly against the front of the Bentley – just to make sure he didn't notice the chain. Which, given the amount of time he usually gave to noticing himself, was not very likely.

'Nice little car this,' he says to the girl as she tugs her skirt as close as it'll get to her knees. 'Not many of these about.'

And just as he starts it up, he says something that really creases me. I had to kick the Drummer to stop him guffawing.

'It rattles a little!'

Rattles. Mate, you ain't heard nothing yet.

He gave the motor a little rev, let his foot off the clutch and raced away. Behind him the chain paid out, and there must have been a good length of it because he was in second gear and touching twenty when it went taut.

BANG! SNAP! MAGIC!

I couldn't believe my eyes – The Fly's car was torn in half! Jack Jay's Bentley was still sitting there with the Drummer leaning against it (I'd moved to a safer spot) and the back half of the little car was still attached to the chain. But the front half, with The Fly and the bird from the chorus line, was another five to ten yards further on, its nose pointing skywards at an angle of forty-five degrees and the bird tugging even more fiercely at her skirt. It was the funniest thing I'd ever seen.

The Fly didn't think it was funny, of course. He threatened to take me to court at one stage, but Jack talked him out of it. After all, I was a star of the show and he was doing good business that summer.

Less destructive, but almost as funny, was the joke a group of us played on a floor manager at London Weekend Television studios, where I was working on a new series. Although it was my own series, that didn't stop me larking about with the studio hands rather than hobnobbing with the high-fliers. The way I looked at it, my life – or at least my career – was in their hands when I was on camera, so I made sure they were on my side. It's a bit like being a singer. You make sure the musicians are with you, not against you.

Consequently, because I was always playing gags with the guys, I made life somewhat hectic for the floor manager. Not that he didn't deserve it, although I suppose when you're dealing with loonies like me you have to be nasty sometimes or nothing gets on video. However, he'd upset a few other people as well, and during the course of a party to celebrate finishing the show, a group of us got to talking about pulling some little stunt on him.

It was the set boys who had the bright idea and carried it out. My job was to nobble the FM and keep him talking for at least an hour. Well, given our relationship over the previous couple of months, that was expecting too much. So I kept an eye on him while he was doing the rounds, and when it looked as if he was leaving I nailed him for a little chat: thanked him for all he'd done, apologized for larking around so much and got him another drink – or two.

'Thanks all the same, Joe, but I really must go now.'

'Just one more and I'll come along with you.'

(I wasn't going to miss the fun.)

Eventually we made our way to the car park, one of those multi-storey jobs. Only his car was nowhere to be seen. Instead, where he'd left it earlier that day was this little construction made of bricks: no windows, no doors, just a compact brick cube. What the set boys had done was build this thing around his car with quick-drying cement. It took four of them just over two hours, they told me later. It took two or three times as long to remove it, chipping it away brick by brick, and all the time the floor manager's saying 'Mind the paintwork. Mind the paintwork.'

It was some time before I went back to London Weekend – and not by car.

Not that I lost much sleep about that. As a musician I never liked television a lot. For one thing, it was all so impersonal. It took away, to a large extent, the feeling of performing *to* an audience, leaving you with the feeling that you were performing *at* them. Not that this seemed to bother the directors and producers, who as long as they got you on their screens – and rooted firmly to the inevitable chalk mark – were quite happy. The actual performance never seemed to matter.

As to the sound – forget it.

I was once told by a director's assistant at the BBC that only thirty per cent of people actually *listened*. The worst thing was that she believed it.

To be fair, though, I must say that the time the sound engineers were given to get it right was nothing to the time spent on the visual side. It's only in recent years, after the trouble people like myself have made over sound reproduction, that things have improved. I'd say that out of all the arguments I've had with television people, ninety per cent have been about sound problems.

Once, on an early rock show, the boys and I played a little gag to bring this home.

'Listen,' I told the lads, 'when we get two bars out of the middle eight, everyone stop singing and playing. Just mime it till we get to the next verse. OK?'

Off we went. I could see the vision director sitting in his box behind the soundproof glass, intent on his pretty pictures. In the next box along sat the sound engineer, looking bored. That was soon to change. We came out of the middle eight and as arranged all stopped singing and playing. Just miming. The sound bloke's head went up and he looked through the glass at us. To all intents and purposes we were working away as usual. He turned to his assistant, who just shrugged, and began fiddling furiously with knobs and faders, obviously trying to raise the non-existent volume. By the time we'd mimed our way to the verse, he must have been at full level.

WHAM! In we came again, all looking angelic as though we didn't know what was going on. The sound crew were stone deaf for a week. The vision bloke didn't even notice.

18 Pantomime

'Nice little gig,' said George. 'You can stay with Vicki's folks in Liverpool and save some money.'

'Where is it?'

'Some place in New Brighton. Brian Epstein's putting on a show there with some of his bands. He wants you to top the bill.'

Nice little gig! The 'band' we followed was The Beatles and it was pandemonium. Screaming, yelling, the place was alive. All I can say is that we managed to hold the stage with a good set. But I knew that was it. I'd seen the writing on the wall. It was time to start looking in new directions or I wouldn't just be a fading pop star. I'd be back firing engines – and there wasn't much future in that either. They were all diesels by then.

The stage was one answer. I'd already done one pantomime, enjoyed the atmosphere and liked the pros I'd worked with. Being star of the show helped, of course, though to be honest I knew only too well that as far as talent and experience went I had no right to be. It was simply the way things were: find a pop star who could just about tie his own bootlaces and hang a show on him, using his name to pull in the kids and fill the houses. The pros would carry the production.

The pantomime I'd done was *Aladdin* at the Globe Theatre in Stockton-on-Tees. I was Wishy-Washy – a cockney Chinaman. The worst kind of all. Bleedin' nice, I thought. All my dialogue'll be in numbers. Number 23, number 32, number 8 but light on the sweet and sour. Music by Lionel Bart.

The show was produced by Cyril Dowler, who together with George Bolton put me up some time later for the Grand Order of Water Rats, a

The Grand Order of Water Rats.

show business charity organization, which I might add I'm very proud to be associated with. Bud Flanagan was King Rat when I joined, and having once spent every free night watching the Crazy Gang, the night I was initiated into the Order was one of the great moments of my life.

George Bolton, a lovely man, one of the great dames of the British stage, introduced me to a world of comedy that I'd begun to think was corny, and it wouldn't be going too far to say that the season I spent with him in Stockton-on-Tees changed the way my professional life was heading. He'd done something like forty-two pantos when I met him for his forty-third, so I tended to look at him with some awe. For one thing I thought he might have been put out at having this smart-alec rock and roll singer coming into his first panto and topping the bill. Not a bit of it. He couldn't have been nicer.

'Come to my room, dear boy, and meet the wife.'

There in his dressing-room was Freda, a very pretty lady with a beautiful big smile, ironing one of George's dame's dresses. The room smelt of make-up: not the pancake stuff we rockers had taken to using on television but the proper old-fashioned Leichner grease sticks that you had to remove with cold cream. Talk about backstage atmosphere –

George Bolton, one of the great dames of the British stage, playing Widow Twankey in Aladdin.

the whole theatre reeked of Leichner No. 5 and No. 9. But what really caught my eye were the crates of Guinness, boxes of sweets and crisps and cases of all kinds of goodies packed along one wall.

'Perks, dear boy, perks,' he told me when I asked about his own little Aladdin's cave. 'I tell them I'll do a gag about Guinness, they send me a crate of the stuff. Doesn't get a laugh, but the dressing-room's full of it. As you can see. I nearly got myself a bike as well last year, but I said to the man, "I'm too bloody old to ride it. Send me some sherry instead." '

The memory produced a raucous laugh.

'We all do it, you know. All the old pros. Ring around the local firms where you're playing and offer to give them a plug on the show in return for a little contribution. But it never gets a laugh.' He wiped his eyes. 'I mean, dear boy, who'd laugh at the mention of a Mars Bar?'

He roared with laughter again. Here, I thought, is a bloke with a sense of humour. And what a lovely life, touring with his lovely wife to iron his costumes, dress him and look after him.

'A little glass of sherry, George,' Freda would say before he went on. 'A little glass of sherry's good for the throat.'

All the time I worked with George I never knew him do or say anything in bad taste. Unlike some of the blue gags they use nowadays to get a laugh. As far as the stage is concerned they're the nails-in-the-coffin of variety. George, however, would never stoop so low – unless he was going to 'nanny-goat' you. He'd bend double, paw the ground with his feet and charge right at you. Generally when you weren't looking. At any time in the show. It was like a running gag with George. I almost had him in the pit one night by sidestepping at the last minute, but he put on the anchors, straightened up and went right into his 'Li-ti-tiddle' routine, dancing away as if nothing out of the ordinary had happened.

Early in the show we shared an exit, and the first night I thought he'd lost his marbles, the way he was jabbering on to me.

'How goes it then, my lad? Good or bad? Up goes the brush, down comes the soot. Six, nine and a bob. All jelly takes the wrinkles out of your Aunt Nellie. What can't speak can't lie. What I always say is your mother should have kept . . .'

By which time we'd be in the wings.

'George, mate! What are you on about?' I asked him on the way down to the dressing-rooms.

'It's called talking-off, dear boy. Keep on talking as you come off and the audience think they're getting their money's worth.'

Marvellous man. He saw me looking troubled one day, towards the end of the season.

'Dear boy, you look worried. What's the matter?'

To tell you the truth, I was worried. Keeping one ear to the ground and the other open to the weather, I'd come to learn that as one of the stars of the show I'd have to tip everybody at the end of the season: the lighting team, the sound blokes, stage hands, orchestra, musical director and whoever else helped keep the show going. It being my first panto, I wanted to do this right, but I wasn't sure how to go about it. Too little and I'd be remembered as a mean bastard: too much and I could embarrass the others in the cast. It was a small point, but worrying about it was getting to me.

George put me at ease immediately. 'Dear boy,' he bellowed in a cutting stage voice, 'you must do as I will do.'

'What's that then?'

'I shall give the band leader my kind regards and on my way out I shall show the doorman a shilling.'

Another pantomime veteran on the same show was Johnny Clayton, one of the nicest little blokes I've ever met. He played the Genie of the

Lamp, which gave him three good lines in the whole panto.

Line one: 'I am the Genie of the Lamp. What is your command, O Master?'

Line two: 'I am the Genie of the Lamp. What is your command, O Master?'

Line three: 'I am the Genie of the Lamp. What is your command, O Master?'

Hardly a taxing part, but he did get to wear a loin-cloth, a turban and very little else. Which is probably why, given that the panto season comes in the middle of winter, Johnny's speciality was a fire-eating act. He'd fill his mouth with this dreadful homemade concoction of paraffin, ether and God knows what, and when Aladdin rubbed the magic lamp he'd dash on stage carrying his tar-sticks (small pieces of lit, tar-coated wood) which he'd breathe over, sending a spectacular sheet of flame across the stage. From where the audience sat, it looked as if the flame was coming right out of his mouth.

Up would strike the orchestra and Genie Johnny would go into his eastern dance routine during which, as well as doing some more flame-throwing, he'd burn himself all over. Very impressive it was – little bright sparks would shoot off his skin because he used to cover himself with iron filings. Very uncomfortable, I'm sure, but then so too were the flames from his tar sticks. Many a night I stood in the wings listening to his little cries of agony mixed with pleasure.

'Oh, the pain, the pain! Oh, the pain!'

This exquisite torture would go on for six or seven minutes – long enough to sort out the children from the parents – after which he'd shake the tar sticks on to the stage, stamp out all the little blobs of flaming tar with his bare feet, and utter his first immortal line.

'I am the Genie of the Lamp. What is your command, O Master?'

He never fluffed it. A true professional.

What Johnny hadn't reckoned with were the Jobsworths of Stockton-on-Tees. They didn't fancy the idea of little blobs of burning tar falling on the dry wooden stage of the Globe Theatre: and who could blame them? Poor Johnny was heart-burnt. Every day at rehearsals he pestered Cyril to let him do his little act. He begged, he pleaded, he cajoled, he would have bribed him if we'd been getting paid regularly. Not that Cyril needed convincing. He knew that Johnny's was the best way to ignite the audience when Aladdin first rubs the lamp. But fire regulations are fire regulations. Johnny came to me. I was the star of the show; couldn't I have a word with Cyril? In the end he wore down all opposition and, after a lot of argument with the Jobsworths, we obtained permission. Johnny was back in action – provided there were always two firemen present when he did his act.

So there we were. Aladdin would be thrown in the cave by Abanazar.

Everybody boo.

He/she would sing a dreadful song – 'You'll Never Walk Alone' – and then discover the lamp, pick it up, utter the dramatic words: 'What a dirty old lamp! What you need is a good clean.'

Rubs the lamp and out jumps Johnny with his Molotov mouth and his tar sticks: whoosh of flame and a quick pirouette to display the loin-cloth and turban in all their glory. Very fond of that loin-cloth, Johnny was. It meant he could get more pain up the backs of his legs, so proving his dedication as an actor. He obviously equated burnt legs with the agony of being shut up in an old brass lamp for two thousand years. It's called method acting – and there was madness in his method.

Come the fateful night.

Abanazar had just thrown Aladdin into the cave and delivered his speech: it was so villainous it was one of the highlights of the pantomime, with everybody booing him. Aladdin did her rotten song – not so much a rotten song as the way she sang it really – and her theatrical eye came to rest on that wonderful item of magic: to wit, the dirty old lamp. This was Johnny's cue. He filled his mouth with his evil cocktail and lit his tar sticks, closely watched by two nervous firemen. Surrounded by off-stage canvas scenery and curtains, he was, to say the least, a dodgy number. Because once the tar sticks were lit, the only safe place to put them out was on the stage itself, where there was plenty of room. Furthermore, taking into account that it was the vapour that ignited, not the actual liquid, the only time Johnny had before he did his bit was as long as he could hold his breath.

On stage, meanwhile, Aladdin has picked up the lamp and is looking at it. Whereupon some impatient little bleeder in the audience shouts 'Rub the lamp!' He'd seen the show before and couldn't wait for the appearance of the genie with the tongue of flame.

What happens? The silly cow, instead of getting on with it, and probably because it's the only reaction she's managed to raise in the whole season, decides to ad lib – a privilege afforded only to the likes of George Bolton, who knew what he was doing. As soon as that kid shouted 'Rub the lamp!' a vision of stardom glinted in her eye.

Holding up the lamp and stepping majestically forward to the footlights, she flung both arms wide and shouted, 'What shall I do with this dirty old lamp?'

The kids took up the cry.

'Rub the lamp! Rub the dirty old lamp!'

Her face was glowing. Recognition at last – an opportunity too good to be missed.

'This side shouted louder than that side,' she screamed, waving her arms from side to side as the kids responded enthusiastically, their little faces glowing red with excitement. In the wings Johnny's face was going blue with asphyxiation. The two firemen couldn't decide whether to make him swallow the stuff or to run like hell for safety. As for me, watching from the wings opposite, I couldn't believe what was happening. The audience were screaming 'The lamp! The lamp! Rub the dirty old lamp!' And bleedin' Aladdin's standing there with a silly grin on her face as if she'd just won the pools.

Until, at long last, with the lamp in her right hand, she slowly, teasingly brings both hands together and just touches the lamp.

WHOOSH!

Me as the gypsy guitarist in Aladdin *at the Theatre Royal, Windsor, for the 1985–6 season.*

Johnny burst on to the stage belching flame. It was spectacular. Professionally it was perfectly placed. Which unprofessionally Ad-libbin' – sorry, Aladdin was not. She'd come downstage too far in the hope of furthering her career – which now went up in smoke, literally, catching the full blast of Johnny Clayton's imminent asphyxiation.

When the smoke cleared she stood there like something from a Tom and Jerry cartoon, black from head to foot. Her eyebrows had disappeared and the rim of her Chinese straw coolie's hat was smouldering away like a burnt-out Catherine Wheel. Through it all the dirty old lamp glinted defiantly. The kids were beside themselves. Still Aladdin stood there, squinting through singed eyelashes at the lamp as if *it* were the real cause of her misfortune. Finally, with a stamp of her foot, she hurled it at the orchestra leader and stormed off, leaving Johnny to touch himself up with his tar sticks.

19 Charlie Girl

Charlie Girl was a musical: a direct steal from Cinderella, really, even down to the names of the characters. Anna Neagle's part, Lady Hadwell, was based on the pantomime's Baron Hardup, while my character, Joe Studholme, was Studs for short – and for Studs read Buttons. Oh yes, it was clever stuff. There were two pretty sisters with ugly temperaments, and of course Cinderella was Charlie Girl: when she wasn't Christine Holmes, who became Christine Sparkle, who in her spare time found time to write a couple of hit songs, including 'Devil Woman' for Cliff Richard. Jack Connor was the name of the American prince who was swept off his feet by Charlie Girl, though in the end her head, heart and hand were won by common old Joe Brown. But more of that later.

In those days – we opened at the Royal Adelphi theatre in December 1965 – it was a big achievement for a pop singer to appear in a West End show, let alone top the bill – and get the girl. Yet strangely enough I'd been involved with the show almost from the time Ross Taylor conceived the idea as a spoof on Cinderella. Anna Neagle came to see me about it the year I was doing that summer season on the pier at Yarmouth, and between then and *Charlie Girl* opening I'd married Vicki, and Samantha, our daughter, had been born. Pete, our son, was born while I was in the show.

To say I was nervous about appearing in a West End production would be an understatement. I was bleedin' petrified, and I don't know how I'd have managed if it hadn't been for the professional help and kindness of people like Anna and Hy Hazell. They were terrific: and that's a lot more than can be said for the critics. We were SLATED like

Vicki and me with Samantha, and Pete who was born while I was in Charlie Girl.

you wouldn't believe. I think the only good notice I got came from the *Daily Worker*, the Communist paper, which praised Joe Brown's 'working-class vitality'. Thank God me mum never sent me to Eton 'n' 'Arrow.

The looks on the faces of the cast when the papers came in – despair isn't the word for it. We'd had the traditional first-night party, everyone letting off steam after the nervous tension, bitching and excitement that leads up to a first night, but when the papers arrived and we read the reviews, everyone's faces crumpled. We opened on 15 December, and we all wondered if we'd still be working after Christmas. But it goes to show that reviews don't always mean a lot, except to an actor's ego, because *Charlie Girl* ran for five or six years and went on tour in Britain and overseas.

A great deal of the credit for the show's survival must go to Harold Fielding, the executive producer. He was a very sharp man, as shown by the fact that Larry Parnes was associated with the production. You could rest assured that the Parnes wouldn't get involved with somebody who wasn't going to bring him a bob or two. The day after the bad press, there was a crisis meeting at which Harold Fielding came up with an answer. If the principals would agree to a cut in wages, the money saved would be used to promote the show. We agreed and the promotion campaign worked – the show was saved and we kept our jobs. At the time I did ask my manager if I could have something in return for a cut in wages, and he negotiated with Fielding for me to have six free tickets to be used by a certain time. Unfortunately I didn't use them by that time, and when I asked some months later for my six free tickets he refused to give them to me. That was the last time *I* took a cut in wages.

Another lesson I learnt from being in *Charlie Girl* was the art of upstaging. I'd heard the word used, but I never really knew what it meant until I met Derek Nimmo. He was Lady Hadwell's butler. There I was one evening, singing one of my numbers, when Derek danced along right in front of me, carrying his balloons and swinging his brolly. I couldn't see the audience, which meant the audience couldn't see me.

'Do that again, mate, and there'll be trouble,' I told him.

He did do it again and there was trouble. I stuck out my foot as he went waltzing past and almost up-ended him into the orchestra. Next thing I know I'm up before Harold Fielding and Wallace Douglas, the director, and in big trouble. Derek thought that was a great laugh, and it wasn't long before I saw the funny side of it as well.

But then Derek wasn't the sort you could hold a grudge against for long. He had such a good sense of humour: and he had the cheek of the devil. As anyone who's been to a West End theatre knows, the worst problem is finding somewhere to park. It's hopeless at night and impossible if it's a matinée. Not for Derek, though. He'd come in each day in this lovely old Bentley of his and drive straight into the car park of the Air Ministry, which was near the Adelphi. Immediately he'd be set upon by a Jobsworth, but before the lackey could open his mouth Derek would put on his bowler hat, take his brolly and briefcase from the car, instruct the Jobsworth to 'Look after this car for me, my man,' and march confidently through the front door of the Air Ministry building before the Jobsworth had time even to salute. Once through the front door, it was only a quick nip down a corridor, out through a back door and across the road into the stage door of the Adelphi. You had to hand it to him.

We had four stage villains in the show: but one day a couple of real-life villains did over the dressing-rooms while we were all on stage. All kinds of things went missing – money mostly, but also personal things which are much harder to replace. Anna, for instance, lost a lot of very good costume jewellery that she'd put together over the years. And some of her china cats. It was well known among her fans that she collected these china cats, and they'd send litters of them round to the stage door for her. Everywhere you looked in her dressing-room would be china cats. Happily for Anna, and for the rest of us, the police caught up with these two and recovered most of the loot, which they itemized and sent the list to everyone in the cast so we could come and identify what we'd lost. It was quite a laugh, because on it they'd included a packet of Durex. Much hilarity was had by all, guessing whose pocket that had been nicked from. But even funnier was the comment I heard as I was passing Anna's dressing-room. She was in there with her husband Herbert Wilcox, reading through the list.

'Oh look,' I heard her say, 'they even found the Durex you used to glue on my pussy's head.'

She was very nice and very kind, but she could be wonderfully naïve at times.

Rehearsing for Charlie Girl *with Dame Anna Neagle.*

The four villains in *Charlie Girl* were stuntmen rather than actors. They livened up the action by breaking into Lady Hadwell's mansion and there were some good fight scenes. Tony Oakman, who'd been my guitarist in the Bruvvers, got a job as one of the stuntmen and stayed in the show longer than I did. But in the first place he'd come along as my dresser: not much of a job for a good guitarist, and to be honest I didn't need a dresser. On the other hand I had to do something for Tony. He'd been with me at the very start but had missed out on a lot of the fun by getting called up to do his National Service in the RAF. When he came out two years later we had another guitarist, and even when Tony did finally come back into the Bruvvers, it wasn't long before I went into *Charlie Girl*.

At first I thought I was doing him a favour by taking him with me, but before long we realized that his being my dresser was demeaning for both of us. We were too close to fall out over it, but the situation did put a strain on our friendship. It was a relief, then, when he came in one day with news that one of the stuntmen was leaving the show and he was hoping to get his job. He'd learnt all the stunts. Could I put in a word for him with Wally Douglas?

Wally agreed to give Tony an audition (anything to get me off his back) and called him up to his office.

'So you want to be a stuntman,' he said to Tony. 'Ever been a stuntman before?'

'No,' said Tony, 'but I've learnt all the stunts in the show.'

'All right then. Let's see you do a forward roll.'

Tony looked at him. At no time in the show did one of the stuntmen have to do a forward roll. What was worse, at no time in his life had Tony ever done a forward roll. However, there was a part at stake. He had a go and made a terrible hash of it, hitting his head hard on the floor as he turned over. As soon as he got up, Wally made him do some other things – flips and rolls – and while poor Tony made a fool of himself, Wally just sat there laughing at him. I was furious, but what could I do? Wally said, 'He's not a stuntman,' and that was the end of the argument.

Eventually another stuntman left, and this time I made sure Wally played it straight.

'Tony knows the stunts and he knows the show. He's keen. Give him a proper chance this time.'

Wally, to his credit, did just that and Tony got the job. Moreover he had a speaking part. Only one line, admittedly, but that one line changed his personality. When the four villains were casing Lady Hadwell's, Tony's job was to write down the items they'd need for the robbery.

Rope, jemmy, swag bag, that kind of thing. One of the other villains would then say, 'We mustn't forget those guard dogs,' and Tony would say, as he wrote it down:

'Six pounds of best steak.'

But he had to say it so that it could be heard throughout the theatre, and there were no microphones. So every night old Tony would bark at the top of his voice:

'SIX POUNDS OF BEST STEAK!'

Years later, whenever I saw him, he'd come up to me and boom:

'HELLO, JOE. HOW ARE YOU?'

He was quite unable to speak quietly any more. It was amazing.

I had voice trouble as well because of *Charlie Girl*. I wasn't used to singing without a microphone, and after several months of projecting my voice, it began to give out on me. First of all they sent me to a voice therapist called Arnold Rose, who was said to be good. He had a special way of teaching you to sing, such as making you grunt from the back of your throat. Fat lot of good that did me. Next I went into hospital to have my tonsils out – and that didn't make any difference.

'One of the problems,' I said to Joan Preston, who was Harold Fielding's right-hand woman, 'is that I'm having to struggle to make myself heard over the drummer. Maybe it would help if we could get him to quieten it down a bit.'

It's not that he was a bad drummer: far from it. He used to be Billy Cotton's drummer. So we had a little meeting with the musical director, at that time a bloke called Donald Elliott, who'd had a lot to do with ballet and opera.

'Oh, the drummer doesn't concern me,' he said. 'Drumming has absolutely nothing to do with music.'

'What does it have to do with then?' I demanded.

'If you want my opinion,' he answered coolly, 'drumming is a personal sport.'

Knowing drummers the way I do, I had to admit he had a point. But it didn't help my voice, and in the end I left the show rather than run the risk of further damage. Looking back on it sometimes, I'm surprised they never asked me to leave anyway. I was never your traditional West End actor.

I remember one matinée when I came right out of character and addressed an old dear sitting in the front row. She'd obviously seen the show before, and this afternoon she was telling her friend, in a loud voice we could all hear on stage, not what was happening so much as what was going to happen. It was incredibly distracting, but we went through the whole show with her until it came to the climax. This was when I was about to go away and had come to say goodbye to Charlie. It was all very sad because of course we loved each other truly but neither was aware of the other's feelings. Something like that anyway. Charlie had earlier said that when she kissed the man she loved she would hear bells ringing, and when I kissed Charlie goodbye, the drummer (good fellow) did a little peal of bells on his triangle. True love and all live happily ever after.

This particular afternoon we were at the farewell scene and I was about to cross the stage to kiss Charlie goodbye when the woman's voice boomed through the sad and silent theatre.

'Now 'e kisses 'er!'

Halfway across the stage I stopped, turned and looked straight down at her. Joe Studholme became Joe Brown.

'Turn it up, Mrs,' I said. 'Let the dog see the rabbit.'

It brought the house down.

20 The budgie man

The lengths to which some people will go to make their show business career take flight are quite astonishing. Frightening, too, at times. Such as the night I came home from playing in *Charlie Girl* to find Vicki in a state of agitation. She'd answered a knock at the door and was immediately surrounded by a flock of budgerigars.

'Who was it?' I asked.

'I don't know. When I opened the door, all these birds flew in all around me, like in that Hitchcock film, and this fellow was standing on the doorstep playing the mouth organ. I asked him what he wanted and he said he wanted to see you. It took ages to get rid of him, love. In fact I was quite rude to him in the end.'

'Don't worry about that, mate. We'll probably never hear from him again.'

How wrong can you be! Several nights later, a Sunday it must've been, I was sitting at home on my own, waiting for Vicki to get back from a late recording session, when the doorbell rang. It was a bloke of about thirty, well dressed, very polite, asking if I could spare him ten minutes of my time.

'Certainly, mate,' I said. 'Come on in.'

Wrong again.

I led the way into the sitting-room and invited him to sit down.

'What can I do for you?'

'Well,' he said, 'I know you must get hundreds of people like me bothering you, but the truth is . . .'

In a twinkling his manner changed from that of the polite uninvited guest to that of a circus barker.

'THIS IS YOUR LUCKY DAY!'

Not at ten o'clock on my night off, it wasn't.

'I've got an act that could take the known world by storm.'

'Hang on a minute, mate. I'm not an agent. I'm just a performer myself and I've got enough problems with my own act.'

'Point taken, squire, point taken. But *this* act you've got to see.'

My momentary silence he took for assent.

'Now,' he continued, 'you just sit there and leave the rest to me.'

Off he went towards the front door, leaving me wondering what I'd let myself in for. I still hadn't connected him with the Budgie Man who'd scared Vicki – but I was about to. Back he came carrying a large cage, full of the birds, and a small cardboard suitcase. Then, without so much as a who's a pretty boy, he opened the cage. In ten seconds the room was full of flying budgies.

'I did this act the other evening for your cleaning lady, squire, but she wouldn't know a good act if you pasted it to the tip of her nose. Silly cow told me to piss off.'

I didn't mind my wife using bad language, but I did object to her being called a silly cow. After all, it was a reflection on my judgement. However, I thought better of slinging him out. Not that he'd have been any trouble. But what would I do with all those bloody budgies? I let it ride.

'Watch this,' he said, opening the case and taking out a large mouth organ. No sooner had he begun to play than half a dozen birds landed on his head. He stretched out his right arm, blew a few more notes, and more birds perched on the proferred limb. Reaching into the case with his free hand, he took out an even larger mouth organ on which he blew the most awful rendition of 'Swanee River' you've ever heard. The birds loved it. They were going frantic. The room was full of blue and yellow feathers and bird shit.

'My cleaning lady's not going to like this,' I told him.

'Bet your wife would love it, squire.'

I cringed. This bloke was getting on my nerves. It was time to call a halt.

'Look, get the birds back in the cage and we'll talk about it.'

He stopped playing. Immediately they all flew straight to the cage and settled *on the roof*.

'What do you think of that then, squire?'

'Different. And not so draughty.'

He shot me a funny look.

'Ah. But you've seen nothing yet. You just wait there a minute.'

He shot off through the front door, leaving me staring in disbelief at the budgies on the bird cage. Then I heard him returning and he was talking to someone. Oh lord, I thought, he's got a parrot as well. No, it was a person.

'Come on, come on,' he was saying. 'I think he's getting pissed off.'

There was some banging and scuffling in the hall, and next thing this slim, pale, harrassed-looking woman staggered into the room, sagging under the weight of a huge packing-case. Behind her came the Budgie Man, prodding her in the bum to hurry her along.

'This is the wife,' he announced by way of introduction. She won my immediate sympathy.

'Hello, mate,' I said. 'Sit down.'

Without a word she sat at the far end of the sofa from me. The Budgie Man plonked himself between us.

'Go on, go on,' he said to her. 'Get it out. Get it out.'

She went over to the packing-case and began to unpack it, during which he and I became involved in one of those strange conversations in which the third person in the room is discussed as if he or she is not there at all.

'Not bad, is she,' he said. 'How old d'you reckon she is, squire?'

Speechless with embarrassment I was unable to reply.

'Thought that would get you. Forty-two, squire, forty-two. Not bad, eh. Not bad. *And* she's only got one lung.'

I couldn't believe this. I thought she must be deaf, but then I noticed she was nodding her head in agreement.

Eventually she stopped unpacking and began constructing what, when she'd finished, was a strange contraption consisting of some twenty mouth organs bolted together on a single frame. She stepped back from it and they both gazed at it reverently for a few moments.

'Beautiful, innit squire? Bloody BEAUTIFUL! I play that in my act: play that and she stands at the back and does a strip. Right, love?'

She nodded. I panicked. He stood up. I listened. Was that Vicki's car I heard?

'You're not going to do that right now, are you?'

'Thought we might, squire. Let you see the whole act, like.'

'Do me a favour, mate.' I would have been down on my knees pleading with him if there hadn't been so much bird shit on the carpet. 'The cleaning lady'll be here any minute. Just play the bloody thing and get it over with.'

'Righty-oh.' Quite undaunted. 'But first – the string.'

He made a small, theatrical gesture with his hand towards his wife, who slapped a roll of knotted string into his palm – just like a nurse in an operating theatre. This he began to tie, loosely, around his knees, rather like a clothes line: and then he stood on his head! Using his elbows for support he shuffled towards the mouth organs. I looked across at his wife. She still had her clothes on. Any minute now you'll start laughing, I told myself.

'I nick 'em from Woolworths,' the Budgie Man said with a chuckle, nodding towards the mouth organs. When he was close enough to them, he raised himself slightly on his arms and began to play. Immediate chaos. The budgies went crackers, flying round the room again like whirling dervishes, defecating and banging against the windows until, presumably on a given cue, they settled on the string between his knees. He stopped playing. It was over. His wife – I'd forgotten about her – was standing at the other end of the sofa with her blouse in one hand and her bra in the other. The birds returned to their cage.

'What d'you think then, squire? What d'you think?'

'Isn't he wonderful?' said his wife in admiration. 'I'm so proud of him.' She pointed a bra-holding hand in the direction of the mouth-organ contraption. 'He screwed it all together himself, you know.'

Whereupon Vicki walked through the door.

21 The chairman

When I came out of *Charlie Girl* after two and a half years, I went on the club circuit with a ten-piece band and a microphone. The idea was that I'd become an all-round entertainer. Some hope. On the other hand, I did get to meet some of the characters of the show business world: people I might never have met in a thousand years if I'd stayed in the West End.

One such character was Norman Collier, who was a comedian but a very special one in that he would laugh at other people's jokes. Most comedians you meet only listen to you when you tell them a joke, and if they haven't heard it before they mark it up as one they can use in future. Norman wasn't like that. He had a lovely sense of humour and he was a great student of human nature, as was apparent to anyone watching his northern club chairman act. But as Norman once discovered, there are times when it's not easy to distinguish the fiction from the fact.

He arrived late on Sunday morning at a working men's club up north, where he was booked to do two shows: one in the afternoon and one in the evening. The place was deserted, so Norman – typical of the bloke he is – sat in the car park and waited. Eventually, just as he was dozing off, there was a tap on the car window and Norman found himself face to face with the epitome of his own club chairman character. He wound down the window to let in a rush of boozy breath that said,

'Thee must be Norman. I'm club Chairman.'

'Oh. Yes,' said Norman, being not so much at a loss for words as not being able to find any that seemed suitable for such an occasion.

Being a northerner, and as is their wont, the Chairman came straight to the point.

'Now look 'ere, Norman. Committee and I are sorry thee've 'ad t' come all way for wasted journey, but this afternoon's performance has been cancelled owing to fact t'stripper's got a cold. However, we will be requiring your services at tonight's performance. Good day!'

Having delivered this well-rehearsed speech he turned to go.

'Just a minute,' called Norman. 'What time am I on?'

The Chairman halted, swayed and turned, each act distinct and singular in its execution. He was, Norman decided, even more pissed than he looked.

'Well, Norman. I may call thee, Norman, mayn't I? Good. Well. Clare's turn goes on at eight, then there's darkies at nine and stripper t' follow darkies, and then there's Norman Collier at half ten. That's thee, lad. I'd be 'ere at nine. We're not sure if darkies'll stay on more than five minutes. And stripper's gorgeous lass. From 'Uddersfield.'

'But it's only twelve o'clock,' wailed Norman. 'What am I going to do here all day?' He cast an eye around the mountainous slag heaps. 'Is there anywhere I can get something to eat?'

The Chairman burst into laughter. He appreciated Norman's sense of humour.

'Thee's not in bloody London now, lad. There's a Chinese takeaway in Leeds. I don't know more than that.'

I bet you don't, Norman thought to himself and looked forlorn. The Chairman gazed at him until he'd gleaned sufficient pleasure from the misery expressed on Norman's face.

'Tell thee what. Come 'ome with me and I'll get t' wife to feed thee.'

Norman suddenly knew how a stray dog must feel. The Chairman went round to the passenger's side and dropped into the seat.

'Just follow t'signposts,' he told Norman, and eventually they arrived at a terrace of brick houses, hidden among factories on the outskirts of the town. The Chairman led Norman through the front door and ushered him into the front parlour.

'Stay there, Norman. I'll go and tell the wife.'

He went out, leaving the door slightly ajar. Norman sat down on the edge of the G-Plan settee and waited. He could hear voices coming from down the hall.

The wife: 'Why didn't you warn me?'

Chairman: 'I didn't bloody well know, did I!'

The wife: 'Didn't he bring sandwiches?'

Chairman: 'I'll go and ask him.'

Norman cringed.

The wife: 'I'll come with you.'

He cringed again as he heard their approaching footsteps. In came the Chairman, followed by a woman wearing a floral dress, an apron and tartan slippers.

'The wife,' announced the Chairman, jerking his thumb behind him.

The wife tried to smile and bobbed at the knees in an attempt at a curtsy. Norman stood up while they scrutinized him for signs of a packed lunch.

'I hope I'm not putting you out,' he stammered politely.

The Chairman and the wife said nothing: turned and left the room. Norman perched again on the edge of the settee as outside the room a conversation diminished with the wife's return to her domain.

Chairman: 'I'm sure 'e didn't 'ave any. I told thee that.'

The wife: 'It wouldn't be so bad if Our Jack wasn't coming for Sunday lunch with those two kids. But you know what greedy little beggars they are.'

Chairman: 'Look, just give 'im what thee can. 'E'll need something to keep 'im going. 'E's got t' follow t'stripper tonight, and when she cracks that coconut it wants a bit of following, I can tell thee.'

The doorbell rang.

The wife: 'That'll be Our Jack and kids and I've not done puddings yet.'

Norman heard the Chairman open the front door.

''Ello, Jack, lad. 'Ello there, lads. Come through.'

'It were shame about t'stripper's cold, Dad.'

'Aye. So long as it don't go t'er chest. She's got a promising future ahead of her, that girl. NO, BOYS! Not in there. We've got a visitor.'

Jack and the two boys poked their heads around the door and stared at Norman, who stared at the wall ahead as if he hadn't heard them. The three heads disappeared and the door half-closed again.

'Bloody comedian from club. Found 'im sitting in car park like lost bloody dog.'

The voices became a murmur and faded, leaving Norman in silence and solitude. Ten minutes passed. Another ten and he became aware of two heads staring at him through the crack in the door.

'He's been on telly.'

'No, he hasn't.'

'Bet he has. You ask him.'

'He doesn't look like he has.'

'Come in, boys,' Norman said. 'It'll be nice to have someone to talk to.'

Two bodies followed the two heads into the room. The older one, about nine, was tall for his age, fat, with ginger hair and a crooked nose. His brother, several years younger, was tall for his age, fat, with ginger hair and a running nose. Norman reconsidered the importance of conversation.

''Ere mister,' said the young one. 'You been on telly?'

Norman nodded.

'D'ya get a lot o' money for it?' asked the other.

'Sometimes,' answered Norman.

'Then why are you eating our dinner?' blurted the first.

Norman couldn't answer that. He decided to change the topic of conversation.

'What's your grandfather doing, boys?'

'He's watching match on telly.'

'Well, will you go and ask him if I can speak to him, please?'

That got the kids out of the room. Ten minutes later, presumably half-time, the Chairman appeared, clutching a pint bottle of brown ale. Norman looked at it and licked his lips. The Chairman hid it clumsily behind his back.

'What is it, Norman? Dinner won't be long.'

Norman was about to say something about a drink but changed it to, 'Could you tell me where the toilet is?'

'Aye, lad. Follow me.'

He led Norman through the house to the backyard, at the bottom of which stood the family bog. It was a good one – a smart affair painted green with a corrugated iron roof and a wooden door with gaps at the top and bottom for light and ventilation.

'In there, Norman,' said the Chairman unnecessarily, pointing with his bottle. 'Can thee find tha own way back or shall I wait?'

'No, it's all right,' said Norman. 'You get back. You don't want to miss the match, do you?'

'Bloody right I don't,' said the Chairman, oblivious of the sarcasm.

Norman ventured into the khazi and slammed the door behind him, almost dislodging the long tin bath that hung behind the door from a four-inch nail. He settled down. But squatting there, in man's most vulnerable position, his trousers round his ankles and in his hand a neat square of the *Radio Times* just torn from a two-inch nail in the wall, he became aware of a small pair of tartan slippers poking under the gap at the bottom of the door.

Suddenly they disappeared upwards!

Norman's eyes rose!

Over the door hung a pair of white knuckles.

There was a scrabbling sound and the bath behind the door rattled violently. Between the knuckles appeared the face of the Chairman's wife. Their eyes met.

'I forgot to ask you, Norman. You do like Yorkshire pudding, don't you?'

22 Jimmy Wheeler

Ask anyone in show business about Jimmy Wheeler and you'll hear a funny story about him. Jim was one of the great characters, a good friend of mine, and in a way a very sad case. To say that Jim liked a drink would be a gross understatement, yet when he was on stage, even if he'd had a skinful, he usually managed to get through his spot. And finish with his famous catchphrase:

'AYE AYE, THAT'S YER LOT!'

Only once to my knowledge did he fail to get through his act, and it makes sense of what he used to mutter to me when he was in his cups.

'Son,' he'd say, 'the best place to get pissed is in bed.'

'Why's that then, Jim?' I'd ask.

'Because yer can't fall over, can yer!'

This particular night, Jim was working in a theatre with what's known in the business as a riser, a microphone which is situated, more or less as a solid fixture, just by the footlights in the centre of the stage. It has no loose stand as such but is joined to a rod, which is electrically operated by the stage manager from the prompt corner. When the microphone's required he flicks the switch and up it rises from below the stage until it's at the right height for the act that's coming. It's a bit like a car aerial on posh British motors and most Japanese ones.

Jim, it has to be said, had sunk more than a few bevvies before going to the theatre, but there was nothing unusual in this. Everyone backstage knew that once he was out in front of the audience he'd be all right – though looking at him standing in the wings, breathing deeply and trying to compose himself for the ordeal, you couldn't be blamed for wondering. And this night was different.

'Ladies and gentlemen,' announced the compere, 'Mister Jimmy Wheeler.'

The orchestra struck up and the audience burst into applause: Jimmy inhaled deeply and launched himself on to the stage. He made it to the riser, clutched it for support and almost managed to stay upright. But he was fighting a losing battle. The riser wasn't built for keeping comedians on their feet. Slowly, slowly but surely it began to bend over towards the orchestra who, seeing Jim toppling into their pit in slow motion, stopped playing. By now Jim was struggling desperately to get himself and the riser into a more vertical position. It was too late. He felt himself falling. But just before he went, he had the presence of mind to shout,

'AYE AYE, THAT'S YER LOT!'

Good old Jim. A showman to the last.

Two of my favourite Jimmy Wheeler stories concern the time he was working in a double act with his father. Wheeler and Wilson was the name of the act, and the way Jim told it, the old man was something of a stickler who ruled Jim with a rod of iron.

'There was this show we were doing,' Jim began. 'Can't remember now if it was summer season or panto, but it had a good run, you know.'

Which would explain why Jimmy had time for walking out with a waitress from the coffee shop opposite the theatre. Or, as he said in his own words:

'I was 'aving it orf with this bird in the caff over the road who used to bring our tea and cakes in during the interval. Only that's not all she brought in, is it, 'cause after a couple o' weeks I started to feel a bit of irritation in me old Hampton and I thought,

'AYE AYE . . . this is it. And it was. I'd contracted what is known in yer better classes as a social disease. Not only that, son, but I'd caught a dose. I knew I should o' stirred the tea with a spoon.

'My biggest worry, though, was the old man, 'cause I knew if he found out I'd be in dead trouble. Well, you know how it is – I put up with it for another week.'

'Then one day the father sees me looking peaky in the dressing-room and says, "What's up with you, James? You look a bit off colour. Not eating your cakes, I notice." So I told him. Well, by that time I was past caring. I mean, I hadn't touched a drink for days so I wouldn't have to piss.

'The old man went potty. Stormed up and down the dressing-room. Three yards one way, bumped into a wall: three yards the other way and bumped into the opposite wall. I couldn't tell if he was swearing at me or swearing at the bloke who built the theatre. But what really got me was that it wasn't me he was worried about. Oh no. It was the embarrassment of somebody finding out. As far as my old donga was concerned he didn't seem to care if it dropped off. Come to that, nor did I. It didn't look as if it belonged to me anyway.

'"James, my boy," he told me, "if you think I'm going to let anyone around here sort that out, you are highly mistaken. These things travel like wildfire." As if I didn't know that! "No, my boy, I ain't having everyone put it about that Wheeler and Wilson's a poxy act. *You* are waiting until we get back to London."

'I did, too. And by the time we got back there I was in a right old state, I can tell you. The first morning we was back, the father got himself dressed up in his best bib and tucker and frog-marched me off to the hospital. There we stood in reception, me with me 'ead 'anging down in shame and him all dressed up in his best pin-striped suit with a brushed bowler and his silver-topped cane with his name engraved with diamonds. They must've thought he was one of the hospital directors or some famous Swiss surgeon.

'"Can I help you, sir?" asked the receptionist.

'"Yes," said the father. "My name's Wheeler, this is my son James, and we've come in answer to your advertisement in the piss 'ouse in Leicester Square."'

The other story I like concerns the time Wheeler and Wilson were working the boats, only this time the bird was in the other bed, so to speak. The big liners used to be a good source of income for acts, added to which there was the bonus of a free holiday. Wheeler and Wilson used to do a lot of them in their day, with the result that they were generally well known to the stewards and the crew. 'Even some of the officers spoke to us,' Jim told me.

On one trip, after they'd been at sea for about a week, Jim was approached by one of the stewards, who asked if he could have a quiet word in private.

'You can say it's none of my business, Jim, if you like, but in case you haven't noticed, your old man's taken up with Ma ——.'

The steward mentioned a regular passenger, who was well known to them. Smart and well dressed, very ladylike in her airs and graces, she'd proved to be a bit of a nuisance on most trips, because she too had an act to grind. Hers was to lead prospective suitors a dance, get out of them what she could, then threaten to report them to the ship's captain for molesting her unless some financial agreement could be reached.

Jim thanked the steward for the warning and resolved to tell the father about his new lady friend when the opportunity presented itself. Until then, he kept his eyes open and saw that what the steward had said was true enough. The father had definitely got himself hooked. So he had a word with him: son to father, full of wisdom and experience.

'Don't you worry about me, James, my boy,' said the father, quite unconcerned about Jim's revelations. 'I know what I'm doing.'

The longer the voyage went on, the more Jim wondered about that. Old Wheeler was buying this woman boxes of chocolates, having flowers delivered to her suite, and lord knows what else, and Jim thought it was time for another chat. Got the same reaction. The father knew what he was doing.

'Well, what else could I do? I knew the father was no mug, and he was obviously getting his money's worth as far as the chocolates and flowers were concerned. But I couldn't see how he was going to get out of it before she put the knockers on him.'

The crunch came at a dinner party several days before the ship returned to England. Wheeler and Wilson were guests at the captain's table, along with the lady of the father's attentions and a Sir and Lady Somebody-or-Other. (Obviously important with two hyphens.) Everyone was dressed up to the nines and Jim had been told to act posh and keep his mouth shut. Which must have been hard for the lad because the lady of ill-repute was being very ladylike and hoity-toity: ripe for sending up. As dinner progressed through various courses, the conversation came round to the end-of-voyage fancy dress party. Jim's dad's bird was going on about what she should dress up as, and as Jim put it, 'it was all a bit bloody boring'.

'Tell me, Mr Wheeler,' she addressed Jim's father as if they'd never passed the time of day, let alone the time of night. 'You're a man of the world. What should I do, for I really am in a quandary? As you know, one is not allowed to bring a costume with one. The fun of the occasion is that we all make something up on the spur of the moment, as it were. Come now, Mr Wheeler, you really must help me.'

Which is when Jim saw the sparkle in the father's eye.

AYE AYE, THAT'S YER LOT.

The father looked at the woman, put down his spoon and fork, and leant back in his chair like a man of the world.

'Well, I hope you don't mind my saying,' he said in his poshest voice, 'but you are a dark lady, are you not?'

The woman smiled and went all demure.

'Well, a natural brunette, Mr Wheeler.'

The father paused.

'Then the problem is solved. You can paint your tits and your knees black and go as the five of spades!'

Towards the end, Jim had become pretty disillusioned with the whole of show business, and I can't say that I blamed him. He was treated shabbily by some agents and promoters who, in the past, had made a lot of money out of him. Jim, being a straight bloke himself, couldn't accept this and I know it hurt him deeply. At the same time, though, he never lost his sense of humour and was always ready with an original quip when the occasion demanded it. The last time I saw him on stage was just such a time.

Some bloke from the north of England, who'd done very well with a cabaret club up there, had decided to come to London to try his luck. He'd calculated how much his rent would be, what he'd have to pay in wages and so forth, and he'd come to the conclusion that he could operate in London just as cheaply as he could in Bradford. At the same time, he could charge the punters a considerable amount more. Unfortunately for him, he'd reckoned without the heavy mob, who moved in three weeks after he'd opened, and needless to say the place was closed again inside three months. But not before Jimmy Wheeler had had the misfortune to appear there.

He was booked for the gig by my manager, George Cooper, and on his opening night Vicki, George and his wife and I were there to cheer him on. He certainly needed some support, for the audience were a typical blasé bunch of pissed hooligans and Jimmy, whose act was as clean as a whistle, didn't stand a chance. None the less he got up there with his fiddle and funny gags and did his turn, coming off to mediocre applause and marked indifference.

I was very embarrassed, especially as it was *my* manager who'd booked him into this place. But later, when he came out to join us at our table, he didn't seem all that bothered. He'd been in show business too long to worry over a duff gig and the talk at our table, though initially strained, became good and jolly until we were interrupted by a bawled announcement from the compere.

'Hey, listen here, people!'

People! Whatever happened to ladies and gentlemen?

'Come on, people, listen here. Now you've all had a fair show up to now.'

Bloody cheek, I thought.

'But now it gives me great pleasure, and has done for years, ha ha ha, to introduce you to a young man who has kindly consented to get up here and show us what it's all about. He's had no rehearsal, so please bear with us. I know, I just know, that you are gonna love this.'

No rehearsals, my foot. The bloke got up from his table and immediately went into his act with the band swinging along as if they'd been together for years. This kid did the lot: all the typical Las Vegas shit. Fingers snapping, feet twinkling, impressions, topical gags: he was like an amateur negative of Sammy Davis Junior, only taller. They must have been practising for months to get this right.

I looked across at George.

'What's going on?' I whispered. 'This isn't on. They've already had the star cabaret. This prat should have been on *before* Jimmy.'

George was as much in the dark as any of us. I looked back at the stage. The bloke was JUGGLING.

At this stage I should describe the layout of the club: it was in a long, narrow room with the stage in the centre of one long wall and the audience stretched out either side of it. To give an impression of space, the wall opposite the stage had been fitted with mirrors running the length of the room. We were at a table against the wall on the same side as the stage, and while Vicki and I were facing the stage directly, Jimmy was sitting with his back to the wall, facing the mirrors. So I was looking across him to where matey on stage was now playing the trumpet and tap-dancing at the same time. Any minute now, I thought, he'll be cracking walnuts with his arse. I felt I should say something to Jim.

'Well then, Jim, what do you think?'

I knew what must have been going through his mind. Though talented, this bloke was the epitome of unoriginality. Jim didn't move. He just kept looking straight across the room towards the mirrors. Then finally he spoke.

'He wants to be careful. There's a geezer over there doing his act!'

23 The Great Mandu

I walked into the dressing-room and there, sitting in a chair, stark naked, was a thin little white bloke. That is to say, half of him was white, because standing alongside him, holding a gallon tin of matt black emulsion paint and a five-inch brush, was his brother-in-law. He was painting him!

'Which of you two's the Great Mandu?' I asked.

'He is,' answered the brother-in-law, gesticulating with the brush and sending little splashes of black paint over the walls. The Great Mandu nodded his agreement.

'What do you do, mate?'

Useful to know when you've been lumbered with compering an amateur talent show. First prize was twenty-five quid.

'What does he do? What does he do?' repeated the brother-in-law in tones of awe. 'What *doesn't* he do, you mean. This boy is great. Just GREAT! Right, Dave?'

The Great Mandu stared miserably at the wall in front.

'Well, what sort of act is it? How do I announce him?'

'King of the Fakirs,' said the brother-in-law and I could well believe him. 'Trained in India by the Maharaja of Tandoori. He does the lot – bed of nails, hot coals, meat skewers through the bottom lip. You name it, Dave suffers it. Right, Dave?'

Dave opened his mouth to say something, whereupon brother-in-law slapped a dollop of paint on top of his freshly shaven head.

'Time for the face, Dave. Close your eyes.'

Dave wisely obliged. Brother-in-law dabbed artistically at the left eye socket.

'Good drop of stuff, this,' he said, holding up the tin and studying the label. 'Dries quick as well. Right, one more eye, Dave, a bit of warpaint, and you're finished. Just think of the twenty-five quid.'

I couldn't believe this. I had to ask.

'Look, are you sure he's done this before?'

One white eye opened in panic and immediately closed again to avoid the blackening brush.

'Listen, mate,' said the brother-in-law. 'You just go out and announce a specialty act. We'll do the rest.'

What more could I do? As I turned to leave the room, I could hear Dave whimpering 'How we gonna get the paint off?' and his brother-in-law going on about 'crisp fivers'.

The afternoon was a farce from start to finish – as I should have guessed from the first act. My list said it was a mime act, and when I saw him come out of the wings I thought he looked vaguely like an aged, tatty Tom Jones.

'And who're you going to mime to?' I asked.

'Tom Jones!'

Ask a silly question. Most of the acts were mimes. They'd come on, hand a record to the DJ, and launch themselves into a series of meaningless gyrations in what they believed was a vast improvement on the original. Altogether we had seven Tom Joneses, five Shirley Basseys, two Mick Jaggers and a Mantovani. That bloke just stood there waving a lolly stick at the puzzled crowd. I saved the Great Mandu till last. And eventually there was no avoiding it.

'Ladies and gentlemen, boys and girls. The one we've all been waiting for. THE GREAT MANDU! Let's hear it for him.'

As a few of us put our hands together, the brother-in-law pushed on a large plastic dustbin on wheels which gave off a curious tinkling noise. From where I was standing, it sounded as if it was full of broken glass. It was! Brother-in-law turned to the audience, cleared his throat and bellowed into the microphone.

'LADIES AND GENTLEMEN! In case you think I am the Great Mandu, I am not. I am his personal spiritual adviser. At this moment in time, the Great Mandu is in a transcendental state in preparation for the great ordeal what lays before him.'

Which was a bit naughty considering the Great Mandu was standing in the wings shaking his head vigorously and trying to stop his eyelids from sticking together with the paint – which hadn't dried as quickly as advertised.

I, meanwhile, was dashing round to the audience area. This act I had to see from the front. By the time I got there, the brother-in-law had disappeared, leaving the dustbin standing on its own in the middle of the stage. All around me were people silent in expectation, which is why I could make out, coming from the wings, fierce, aggressive whispers and the occasional whine. The Great Mandu seemed to be needing encouragement to come out of his transcendental state of preparation.

Suddenly there he was, hurtling on to the stage as if he'd been shot from a catapult – or kicked up the arse by an enraged brother-in-law. He stood there, centre-stage, blinking in the footlights, his white, terrified eyes shining out like a couple of hard-boiled eggs in a bucket of treacle. I'd seen nothing like it since the night Ashami stopped playing poker with Mad Menzies.

Finally, with a gesture of resignation to his fate, he reached into the dustbin and pulled from it an empty milk bottle – which he immediately brought down hard on the top of his own head. The crowd gasped! The Great Mandu reeled! The milk bottle remained intact!

The Great Mandu stared in disbelief at the bottle. A great lump had started to rise on his head, producing pinkish-white lines where the skin was stretching but the black paint wasn't. Wham! The Great Mandu hit himself again and still the bottle didn't break. It never would have if it hadn't been for the lump, for next time he brought it down on the lump, whereupon the bottle shattered. And all the time I could hear the brother-in-law exhorting him from the wings.

'Come on, Dave! That's my boy! You can do it! Come on, my son! Once more, Dave, and we're rich!'

But the Great Mandu had had enough. Pre-planned finale or sheer desperation I know not, but without warning he dived headlong straight into the dustbin full of glass. The organist struck a resounding chord and brother-in-law marched on stage to wheel off the dustbin with the Great Mandu's little legs thrashing wildly above the rim. Which is when I noticed that they'd neglected to paint the backs of his legs. It was pathetic.

The brother-in-law excused himself later by saying that he'd seen this James Bond film in which a girl was murdered by having gold paint sprayed over her without leaving a patch for the skin to breathe through. He didn't want that happening to the Great Mandu because he'd just lined up a tour of working men's clubs. I shook my head and gave him the twenty-five quid.

24 Newman rampant

Tony Newman had to be a drummer. A lot of looners are, and Newman was the greatest looner of them all, the most outrageous nutter I've met. The things he did, the things he said, would have landed anybody else in the nick. Not so Newman. He could get away with murder. And he was a great rock drummer: played with Sounds Incorporated who made some records with Gene Vincent. Though that wasn't how I knew him.

Margo, Newman's wife, a long-suffering girl who must have been short on sense, had been a Vernons Girls girl with Vicki: after several years of own goals, score draws and chaperoned gigs, they broke away to form a singing group called, surprise surprise, the Breakaways. Newman and I were thrown together because of the girls and became great pals. Vicki always said that he brought out the worst in me; whenever we were together matters got rather out of hand. It wasn't just the things he did. In fact, it was more the way he did them. He could walk into a room and people would be in hysterics – just like that. He was a very funny man. And a nutter.

Take the time we went to Dublin. Vicki and Margo were backing Clodagh Rodgers at that year's Eurovision Song Contest. Fourteen years later, Clodagh and I were appearing together in a musical called *Pump Boys and Dinettes* in the West End, but that's a different story. Back in 1971 Clodagh was singing the British entry called 'Jack in the Box', a typical load of Eurorubbish designed to brainwash the multitudes. I sometimes think the writers of these songs must spend half their time writing them and the other half on their knees praying for forgiveness to the great god of music. Yet people buy the records!

'Why not come over with us for a couple of days?' Vicki suggested. 'It'll be a nice rest.'

Why not, I thought. And phoned Newman. It was to prove a cardinal mistake.

'Fancy a trip to Dublin for the Eurovision Song Protest?'

'You must be joking,' he retorted. 'I'd sooner watch *Top of the Pops*.'

'No, I'm serious. We could go over with the girls and keep an eye on them. Save them from a foreign entry. Come on, mate. I'll give Dave my drummer a bell and get him to join us. It'll be a good laugh.'

This sniggering sound came down the line.

'Yeah. It might be at that. Righto. I'm in.'

So were Dave and his missus: for better or for worse.

Come the appointed day, we all assembled at Heathrow: not just our little group but Clodagh, musicians, BBC people; in fact, everyone connected with Britain's attempt to win fame and fortune. And that was where the trouble started. Within ten minutes Newman was having false calls put out over the tannoy system for anyone he knew by name: lighting men, sound men, musicians. He was sending them all over the airport, and the more mayhem he caused the more I began to worry about my professional standing with the BBC. Their fat cats weren't going to appreciate half their people rushing about on fool's errands as a result of Newman's anarchic sense of humour. My only consolation was that no one connected it with us – yet. That sense of security disappeared on the coach from Dublin airport to our hotel.

Among the presents Clodagh had been given to commemorate this great event in her life was a large jack in the box, which was being passed around the coach so that everyone could close the lid, open it and be suitably surprised by Jack appearing. For Newman, though, the toy had much greater potential, and when he got his hands on it he reached down into his flight bag for an aerosol can of shaving cream. Holding down Jack's head with a thumb, he filled the whole box with shaving cream, closed the lid, wiped away all traces of cream with his handkerchief and calmly passed the box forward to the BBC producer sitting in the seats ahead. Anyone else would have chosen a production assistant. Not Newman. That wasn't his style. He had to pick on a producer.

Up shot the lid and there sat the producer, covered from the waist up with scented foam. Angrily he snatched off his glasses, wiped them clean and looked about him. Everyone was laughing. End of his options. He gritted his teeth and treated us all to a sickly smile.

'Ha ha, what a wag you are, Tony, to be sure.'

You bloody fool, I thought. Anyone with balls would have stopped the coach there and then and told Newman to piss off. On the other hand he now knew where to lay the blame for a chain of events of which this small frothy incident was but the forerunner. Events that were to put me in the black books of the BBC for years to come. Newman, for his part, couldn't care one way or the other. He never did.

'The day the BBC get a good sound on my drums,' he said to me once, 'is the day I'll start worrying about working for them.'

Being right in the centre of a show business event, yet not actually involved, was a strange new experience for me. I wasn't used to being idle, and what is it they say? The devil finds work for idle hands? Not that he had to find much with Newman around, though the fish hooks were my idea. It was a trick we used to play in the dining-hall at school.

Off we trotted down O'Connell Street: two loony drummers and a gone guitarist: in search of a fishing tackle shop.

'T' be sure 'n' there used to be O'Donnell's in Grafton Street, I'm told.'

Used to be, we said.

'Definitely. Oh yes, definitely. I remember my father, God rest his soul, speaking highly of it to Mr McCane of Blackrock.'

'We've been along Grafton Street,' said Dave.

'An' have you now, though you'll not be finding it. They burnt it down in the Uprising.'

Eventually we found one up O'Connell Street, where we bought a dozen three-pronged pike hooks and a reel of twenty-pound breaking strain nylon line. Back at the hotel, we measured off some line the approximate distance between two tables in the dining-room and fixed hooks to either end. After that it was simply a matter of setting up some drinks and waiting for dinner.

The girls had gone to some reception with Clodagh that evening, so there were just the three of us standing inside the door to the dining-room, waiting to be shown to a table: two drummers and a guitarist who appeared to be tying his shoe laces (on cowboy boots) but in effect was hooking one end of the fishing line to a tablecloth and leaving a neatly rolled coil of line tucked behind the table leg. The Maitre D showed us to our table, left us with the menu and scuttled off to seat a mauve-haired woman on her own.

At the table by the door.

It couldn't have been better. Ten minutes passed: time enough for anyone to notice the fishing line, if anyone was going to, and time enough for Newman to decide on his other victims. No one noticed the line: Newman noticed a family of four entertaining an elderly nun. He got up and went to the lavatory.

Coming back, he dropped his cigarettes. Bending down to retrieve them he also picked up the loose hook. Then he walked over to the table with the nun, paying out line as he went, and asked the man for a light. As he leant over towards the match, his other hand fixed the hook into the tablecloth. Now the almost invisible nylon stretched between the two tables.

Five minutes passed. Heads were bent over soups, lamb cutlets or chocolate mousses. No one stirred: not even a coffee. Where were the waiters? Newman got impatient. He began a drum roll with a spoon on his soup plate: then suddenly stood up screaming,

'WAITER!'

An immense tureen of soup appeared, followed closely by a waiter.

'Just a moment, sir. I'll be with you in a minute,' he said across the room to Newman. And put the tureen of soup on the table occupied by the woman with the mauve hair.

Newman's face lit up with a smile of evil delight. This was too good to be true.

'WAITER!' he shouted again.

'Yes, sir. Yes, sir. Comin' sir.'

He scuttled towards us like a rabbit from a trap – straight into the fishing line. Spurred on by Newman's shouting, his initial momentum carried him farther forward than he would have come had he been walking normally. So he was almost by our table before he realized that *he* had something to do with the sound of falling crockery and cutlery behind him. Even then, it wasn't until he saw the great nickel lid of the soup tureen rolling past him like an empty tortoise that he came to a dead halt and looked around.

His eyes beheld a picture of chaos.

The woman with the mauve hair had just seen her soup bowl disappear in front of her eyes: while at the other table they were, all five, sitting with raised knives and forks staring at the empty mahogany table shining up at them. Both tablecloths were in a jumbled pile on the floor at our end of the room, soon to be joined by a mixture of broth and boiled potatoes.

Enter upon the scene the head waiter, poising for a second to take in the scene before marching towards our hapless fellow with a stern,

'What's all thi . . . i . . . i . . . i . . .'

and promptly slipping head over heels in the soup.

Newman was in hysterics and still screaming,

'WAITER! WAITER!'

But the funniest thing was the English couple sitting opposite us. They ate on as if nothing had happened.

In the confusion that followed, Newman, Dave and I did a quick runner to my room, where we were still rolling around in convulsions when the girls came back. They didn't see the funny side of it. Nor, I'm sure, did the hotel management, though we never heard another word from them about the affair. They probably realized we were to blame and charged it to the BBC, so driving the second nail into my professional coffin. With three more days in Dublin remaining, I began to realize that I could look forward to a set of brass handles as well.

The next evening, following a day of rehearsals for the Eurosongsters, there was the inevitable cocktail party for the Europress. Not having a Eurosong of our own, Dave, Newman and I had spent the best part of the day discussing horses with an Irish barman, who persuaded Newman to part with a fiver on a 'sure ting now'. It was too. Newman came back with fifteen quid which went straight into the drinking fund. So when Vicki and Margo came back from rehearsals to say they'd gleaned some extra tickets for a press reception given by the German contingent, we were very much in the mood for a party. By midway through the evening Newman was reviving his own favourite for Europe. He stood on a table in the middle of the room, wearing a little Hitler tash and singing in a German accent,

'Zer dirty Germans crossed zer Rhine.'

To which we all joined in

'Parlez vous!'

'Zer dirty Germans crossed zer Rhine.'

'Parlez vous!'

'Zer dirty Germans crossed zer Rhine, f––––– zer women and drank zer wine.'

'Inky pinky parlez vous!'

Our German hosts were not amused. We were asked to leave. Whereupon Newman, not to be outdone, dropped his trousers as a parting shot and farted. The Germans – quite reasonably, I thought – complained to the BBC and we weren't invited to any more receptions. Officially that is.

For the next two days, and for the sake of the girls, we kept away from anything Eurovision. We even moved to a different hotel, just the three of us, which is where we met Ronnie Drew, who was one of The Dubliners. These lads were great – local folk heroes – and we went to one of their concerts. Newman kept a very low profile that night, which was wise in the circumstances. Some of the songs were definitely anti-British and alarmingly well received by an audience of big, hard-drinking Irish patriots.

The day after The Dubliners' concert came the Eurovision Song Contest proper. Vicki was dead set for me to go, but as I said to her, there was no way I was going to sit through the same song for three hours. Dave and Newman felt even more strongly about it.

'Anyway,' I told Vicki, 'we've got nothing to wear. It's all tits and tails, isn't it?'

'If you mean it's evening dress,' she said in a voice that fair chilled my Guinness, 'yes, it is.'

'Well, that's it then, isn't it. None of us brought one. Anyway Vick,' I rubbed my hand up and down the bottle to warm it, 'they wouldn't let us in after what happened the other night, let alone invite us to the party afterwards.'

She had to agree that something I said made sense.

'I'll tell you what. We'll stay at the hotel, get some beer in and watch it on the telly. Then we can all meet up afterwards and go for a meal.'

Vicki would've liked to argue about it, but she was already late for a last-minute rehearsal. I let the lads know. They were jubilant.

'But there's one snag. We'll have to watch it on telly 'cause they're bound to ask us about it afterwards.'

'No problem,' said Dave. 'We'll get some beer in.'

We got some beer in. And were doing it justice – the last thing we were doing to the Contest – when there was a knock on the door. I looked at Newman. He looked as mystified as Dave.

'What is it?' he asked as I closed the door.

'It's a big box,' I said, putting it down on the bed.

'P'raps it's a headstone for the career of the git who wrote the Eurosong of the year,' suggested Newman.

I bent over, pulled off the lid and took three steps back as a smell of mothballs escaped from the box. We edged forward and peered inside. Three cards lay on top of scruffy, grey-white tissue paper. Invitations to the post-Contest reception: the Eurobash of the year. And under the tissue paper, three ancient dinner jackets, plus a short, very much to the point letter which, from memory, went something like this.

'Listen, you three bastards. If you don't put these suits on and get yourselves down to the reception tonight, you'll wish you'd never been born. What's more, if you don't behave yourselves, we'll call the police.

(Signed) Vicki.

(Witnessed) Margo and Dave's wife.

I looked at Newman, he looked at Dave, Dave looked at me: we looked at each other forlornly.

'We haven't drunk all the beer,' moaned Dave.

'We'll drink that before we go,' Newman replied.

'We can't go there pissed,' I warned. 'You heard what they said. I know Vicki. She means it.'

Newman, meanwhile, had taken one of the jackets from the box.

'If you think I'm going there sober in one of these, mate, you're highly mistaken.'

He held up the jacket for closer inspection. It was the worst whistle I've laid eyes on: quarter-inch thick dark blue serge with lapels like scimitars which terminated at one huge button below which there was a mere half-inch of cloth. The shoulders were huge, padded, misshapen and shiny grey with wear and age.

'They forgot to bury this one with its owner,' Newman said.

Dave took another jacket from the box and eventually all three were laid out on the bed. We stood back, bottles in hand, surveying them. They were all as bad as the other, except that one was worse. Newman began to snigger: a dangerous sign. It meant he had seen the potential of us turning up at the 1971 Eurovision Song Contest dressed like the three stooges. He changed his tune.

'I want the worst one,' he said.

The jackets were in two sizes: extra large and extra small. Two were extra small, one was extra large. One was navy, one black, the other a greyish charcoal with tatty royal blue silk lapels. In descending order, I was six feet one, Newman was five ten and Dave about five eight. What he lacked in height, Dave made up for in gut. He couldn't get anywhere near the smaller jackets so he had the large one.

It hung from him like an outsize fisherman's cape, the enormous wide shoulders reaching down almost to his elbows while his hands disappeared completely up the sleeves. When he buttoned it, the collar fell back from his neck to his shoulder blades in a wide, greasy arc.

'Très chic,' said Newman.

'Bollocks,' said Dave.

Newman struggled into one of the small ones and gazed in some amazement at the monstrosity in the mirror.

'Hey!' he exclaimed, struck by a thought. 'What about dress shirts?'

We dived into the box.

'Here they are. But they ain't got no collars.'

'Yes they 'ave,' said Newman. 'Them bits of plastic is collars. Bloody 'ell. There's a box of studs and cufflinks as well. Those women aren't giving us much chance of getting out of it, are they. I'll tell you what. If my old lady laughs at me, I'll wring her bleeding neck.'

'I thought you were looking forward to a laugh.'

'So I am, mate. But not from 'er.'

Dave opened three more bottles and we sorted out the trousers. This was getting to be daft. Dave being small waisted, despite his large gut, he needed trousers from one of the other suits, which meant that his jacket was a different colour from his trousers. In the end so was mine; so was Newman's. My trousers came out long in the waist and short in the leg, so I had to drop them as low as the waist would allow, the end result lining up the bottom of the crutch neatly with my knees. With Newman it was opposite: his cuffs almost lined up with his knees.

We opened the last of the bottles, put on the shirts, fought with the studs for half an hour and finally surveyed each other.

We looked awful.

I began to chicken. Time was moving on: and so, as we could see on the telly, was the Eurovision Song Contest.

Suddenly the phone rang.

'Mr Brown? Your taxi's here.'

'I didn't order a taxi.'

'I know,' said the receptionist. 'Your wife did.'

Newman decided it for us.

'Come on,' he said. 'Let's have a loon.'

We went down in the lift and quickly through the reception lobby to the taxi. Dave and I had already piled in when Newman stopped.

''Ang on a minute, I've forgotten something.'

Away he went, returning several minutes later.

'Fish 'ooks,' he said.

'Bloody hell, we can't do that at Dublin Castle. They'll throw us in the dungeons.'

'No they won't. Just tell 'em you're with me.'

Do that, I thought, and they'll incarcerate us as well.

When we walked into the main reception area at the Castle you'd have thought the whole of international show business was there, all done up to the nines. The place reeked of Old Spice and Evening in Paris. No one, we noticed, was wearing conventional evening suits. Come to that, nor were we: but that's beside the point.

'You wait till I get my hands on your missus,' whispered Newman as only a drummer can whisper. Heads turned half a mile away.

'It said evening dress on the tickets,' I said.

'It said evening dress on the box these things came in,' said Newman.

'But look at him – he looks more like a wet Sunday afternoon.'

'Anyway, we're here now. Let's have a look around.'

We mooched off into the crowd. They were all there: the winners, the losers, the posers, the hopefuls. Somewhere in there, too, were some good songwriters who'd forsaken their talent because some greedy publisher had told them it was no sin to make money. They were the saddest of all really, because they were forever apologizing for the fact that they were there at all.

There was one bloke with a nose like the jib of a crane and a small thin moustache.

'Christ,' said Dave, 'if I had a conk like that I wouldn't underline it.'

His suit was royal blue velvet, his shirt pink and frilly, his bow tie huge, black and velvet like a bloated bat. Also round his neck was a large gold medallion. What with that and the nose, he was so top-heavy that he walked with a stoop. As we passed, the bird on his arm was consoling him.

'Don't worry, darling, *I think* your song will be a hit.'

'Please God,' he was murmuring. 'Please God.'

The jacket that was Dave shuffled off in search of a bar. Newman and I walked just behind him, packed into our suits like a couple of Liverpool bouncers. The first drink went down well so we had another. Time passed, the room got warmer, the suits began to react to the heat of our bodies and not even our best friends could have avoided telling us – if we had any friends left.

The smell was becoming unbearable. People were looking in our direction and sniffing disdainfully.

An Italian singer, short and dapper in a spotless white suit and Mediterranean suntan, approached the bar supported by a tall bird on either arm. Newman turned to look them over and the air circulated: the Italian, inhaling through his aquiline Roman hooter, screwed up his face, looked Newman up and down and said something in Italian to the girls. They both giggled and then they moved away in search of fresher climes, the singer holding a handkerchief delicately to his nose. Newman was beside himself.

'Did you see that, Joe?' he demanded.

'See what?' I asked.

''Im. 'Im over there in the white suit. EL BLEEDIN' PIFCO,' he shouted.

'What'd he do?' asked Dave, lowering the ever-present pint.

'Do!' said Newman. 'Do! I'll tell you what 'e did. 'E sniffed at me.'

'I'm not surprised,' said Dave. 'You stink.'

'I know that. You know that. We all bloody stink. But I won't 'ave 'im sniffin' at me, I'm tellin' you. I'll 'ave 'im.'

'Take it easy, mate,' I told him, putting another drink in his hand. 'Don't cause any trouble. Just relax.'

But he couldn't. Ten minutes later he was still smarting. Then his face broke into a huge grin and his hand dropped into his jacket pocket.

'I know,' he said. 'We'll 'ook 'im up.'

'OK,' I agreed. 'But I'd better do it. If he sees you coming he'll smell a rat. No offence, mind.'

We went off in search of El Pifco.

'There 'e is,' said Newman. 'Talking to that priest.'

'Now hang on a minute. I can't go hooking him up to a priest.'

'Why not? 'E shouldn't be 'ere anyway. Look at 'im standing there swigging bloody champagne like altar wine. 'E should be out in the jungle converting cannibals, not poncing around Dublin knocking back free drinks.'

There was no answer to that.

'OK. Give us the hooks.'

Newman handed me a four-feet length of nylon with a hook on each end. I took a deep breath and began pushing my way towards El Pifco and the priest.

Hooking up El Pifco was easy. The poser was standing with one hand in his pocket, so the rear flap of his white jacket stood up nicely. Getting him on the same wavelength as His Reverence was another matter. The priest's evening gown was fairly tight, or put another way he filled it well, and the last thing I wanted to do was stick the hook in him. He might have thought it was the devil prodding him for enjoying earthly pleasures. On the other hand, standing there trying to look cool with a coil of nylon line and a fish hook in my hand, I was beginning to panic. I glanced about to see if anyone was looking at me. Newman was, his neck craning above the crowd and his mouth forming the words ''Ook 'im up. 'Ook 'im up.' There was no way out. I bent down quickly, set the hook about six inches above the hem of the priest's cassock and scarpered. Fast.

This time Newman was prepared to bide his time. Finally El Pifco and the priest ran out of latin they had in common and the priest raised his hand in what could easily be mistaken for a papal salute. El Pifco walked back to his birds, the priest moved off in search of a champagne bottle, and as if by magic the priest's cassock rose to reveal black socks held up by boy scouts' garters with little green tabs on them. Newman was giggling, Dave was drinking, I was fascinated and El Pifco was restrained as if by some heavenly hand. The priest had also stopped, troubled no doubt by the draught. Neither knew what invisible force held them together, and the more they tried to move the more the line took the strain. Pretty soon they were rocking about like performers in some macabre dance. People formed a circle and watched in amazement.

Until some sharp-eyed spoilsport spotted the line.

'Time to go,' said Newman, and we beat a hasty retreat up the great staircase into the hall above. Dave stayed on the stairs to watch the outcome: Newman and I found another bar and got stuck into the booze. It was free, after all. Five minutes later, about the extent of his resistance without a pint, Dave rejoined us.

'What's 'appening?' Newman asked.

Dave could hardly speak for laughing.

''E's tryin' to get the 'ook aht of that priest's 'assock,' he spluttered.

Ten minutes later, Vicki found us. Dave was rolling around the floor wheezing ''E's tryin' to get the 'ook aht of 'is 'assock. 'E's tryin' to get the 'ook aht of 'is 'assock.' Tears were streaming down his face and he was almost choking. Newman, meanwhile, had dropped his trousers and was singing ''Twas on the bridge at midnight' to a group of puzzled continental journalists while I conducted the choruses with a stick of garlic sausage. I looked up and there was Vicki. Across the top of Newman's head I could see divorce staring me straight in the eye.

'Let's go, Tony,' I said, dropping the sausage back on the buffet table. 'It's the girls.'

Ducking down, we worked our way round the table, dragging Dave along with us, until we reached a door. Then we made a dash for the stairs. At the bottom I looked around to see if the girls had followed us and bumped heavily into –

the priest!

He took a long look at me, then at Dave and finally at Newman, who was doing up his fly buttons. That decided him.

'Dat's dem,' he shouted. 'Over here, lads. Don't let dem get away.'

Too late. We were on our way, out of the exit and across the cobbled courtyard. We found ourselves a taxi in Castle Street and headed back to the hotel.

Where the bar was still open.

At two o'clock in the morning.

I didn't know there were so many residents.

Dave got in the beers; an old fellow at the next table got out his cigarettes, felt for his matches and came over to ask Newman for a light. Newman in turn felt in his pockets, but to no avail. The old fellow turned to ask elsewhere.

''Ang on a minute, mate,' Newman said, catching hold of his arm. 'I know I've got some somewhere. Let's 'ave a proper look.'

He stood up and ripped the top pocket of his jacket completely off.

'No. Not there.'

Off came the side pockets. Then the trouser pockets. All eyes were on Newman. The old bloke just stood and gaped at him. By this time Newman was carried away by the ripping time he was having. The trousers were torn from ankle to crutch, the jacket was hanging on him in tatters. Another little old fellow sitting near us was shaking visibly, his knuckles white as he clutched his bottle of Guinness for support. Then came the *coup de grâce*. Newman found his matches.

And set fire to the front of his dress shirt!

The old man dropped his bottle, got up and fled into the foyer, followed by flaming Newman who threw himself full length on the reception desk and began to bawl out one of his obscene songs. Somewhere a camera flashed. It cost me twenty quid but I was lucky enough to get hold of *that* picture later.

Newman, the biggest looner of them all. I had to pay twenty quid to get hold of this picture!

The next day, dressed normally and with nobody talking to us, we boarded the plane along with our wives and the rest of the BBC party. We were a very subdued trio. But you can't keep someone like Newman down for long. About ten minutes before the plane landed at Heathrow, he disappeared into the toilet carrying his flight bag. He emerged dressed in the tattered remains of the evening suit, which he wore all the way through the arrivals area. The last I saw of him – on that trip – he was lying spread-eagled on a circular conveyor belt, going round and round with the suitcases while the porters tried in vain to get him off and Margo was signing up witnesses for the divorce case. Vicki had had enough. She shoved our cases into my hands, grabbed hold of my jacket and marched me out of the terminal into a taxi home.

25 Newman genuant

Only one time did I see Newman come unstuck, and that was at a charity gig, patronized by Her Royal Highness, Princess Margaret, at the Hammersmith Odeon. We – the band and I – were down to do about fifteen minutes. Also on the bill was Donovan (Britain's answer to Dylan), making one of his rare appearances, and this created a lot of interest, particularly among musicians. Newman said he'd like to see Donovan so we took him along as part of our party. Not without apprehension, I might add.

Like most royal charity gigs, this one was hopelessly overbooked and under-rehearsed. Our spot was all right because we were a self-contained unit and didn't have to worry about band parts or arrangement rehearsals. We just went along, got our sound sorted out and disappeared out of everyone's way till curtain up.

Backstage it was murder: people running everywhere, bumping into each other, shouting, screaming, crying, looking for lost props and lost nerve. One poor sod, a ventriloquist, had lost the head of his dummy and was walking round in desperation with his arm stuffed up the back of a mute torso, in danger of becoming the first headless ventriloquist act. Tears streamed down his cheeks as he called out in his ventriloquist's voice:

'Charlie! Charlie! Where are you, Charlie? Has anybody seen Charlie?'

And all the time the piece of broom handle sticking from the dummy's neck kept turning round as if in search of the lost member. It was pathetic.

Our turn came quite early in the running order, and once we'd done our bit there was no way any of us wanted to stay backstage until the end of the show. On the other hand, some of our gear was still on stage so we couldn't just pack up and leave. Dave the Drummer had a brilliant idea – as usual.

'Let's go to the pub and get pissed. Then we can come back in an hour and have a butcher's at Donovan.'

Outside the stage door it was tipping it down, puddles everywhere and black as a coal hole, but when it comes to finding pubs, Dave's like a homing pigeon.

'This way,' he shouted, and we threw our coats over our heads and splashed after him. Sure enough, Dave soon found a boozer, flung open the door in triumph and we all trooped into the saloon bar. Who should be there but Newman, plus a load of other musicians and layabouts, some of whom I knew but hadn't seen for years. They were all obviously well gone.

Newman was standing on a chair with his trousers round his ankles singing one of his own compositions, a charming little ditty called 'Never Rub a Rabbi the Wrong Way Up, He's Liable To Shit Dahn Yer Froat'. The landlord was doing his best to ignore the obscenities as Newman held forth in his accustomed style. No doubt he consoled himself with the fact that he was making a fortune, for this lot were big drinkers and to be tolerated at all costs.

'What are you having, Joe?' someone asked.

'He looks happy enough,' I said, pointing at Newman, who was laughing hysterically at one of his own jokes. 'I'll have the same as him.'

'Right then, one hosepipe coming up.'

Hosepipe? That was a new one on me. I watched the barman who half-filled a pint glass with Guinness, added barley wine, then turned round to the optics and stuck a large brandy in the top.

I took a sip – it was dynamite.

'How many of these has he had?' I asked, indicating Newman who, his trousers completely gone now, was sitting on someone's shoulders in his grubby Y-fronts bawling

'MU-ULE TRAI-AIIN – YAH!'

and banging himself on the head with a tin tray to emphasize the rhythm.

'He's on his fifth,' said the bloke who had bought my drink.

Bloody hell, I thought, having seen Newman work his way through a case of Guinness and still be as sober as a judge. Mad, bad and dangerous, mind you. But sober. Three hosepipes later I was seeing things differently: the whole bar was heaving with people smashing one another over the head with tin trays, laughing and singing Newman ditties.

Back in the Hammersmith Odeon, meanwhile, Donovan was on stage singing 'Mellow Yellow' to his hushed royal audience.

'Oi, Tony!' I yelled. 'We're gonna miss Donovan.'

''Ave another 'osepipe.'

I did. The show finished and we were still looning in the pub when the door flew open and this little bloke in a sodden grey suit and hush puppies sailed into the bar. Soaked from head to foot, he stared open-mouthed round the seething room, frantically wiping away the water that was sliding off his bald head into his eyes. Eventually his eyes found what they were looking for. Me. He squelched over to where two walls were holding me upright.

'Excuse me,' he said, very politely. 'Are you Mr Bwown?'

I nodded.

'Huwwy, huwwy. Come with me. Pwinthess Magawet wants to meet you in the foyer.'

At last, I thought. Me OBE.

I followed him out into the rain, leaving the group and Newman playing Cardinal Puff – a drinking game. Across the road we dashed, and Hush Puppies rushed me up some stairs and into the foyer, where he stood me in a long queue of performers. I was drenched. As the heating in the theatre took effect I began steaming. In front of me was the ventriloquist, wearing a green glitter jacket and still holding the dummy, whose once-missing head now grinned malevolently at everyone. He was still talking to it.

'Now then, Charlie,' he was saying quietly, as if to a child, 'there's nothing to be nervous of. She's only a princess.'

Gradually the queue thinned and at last it was his turn. I moved up alongside to see what the form was. Princess Margaret smiled sweetly at him, and at Charlie, and asked some polite questions. I never saw the poor bloke's lips move: he was so nervous that he did the whole interview in the doll's voice, with the result that an amazed HRH found herself talking to a wooden dummy while the vent looked away in embarrassment. Finally their little chat came to an end, Charlie grinned as malevolently as ever and the vent, remembering the form, bowed. As he did so, he automatically brought his arms to his sides.

And Charlie's head fell off.

As it rolled towards me I gave it a bit of a kick and it disappeared among the legs behind me, its jaws clacking merrily. The vent gave me a malicious look and was moved on. Now it was my turn.

I don't mind admitting I was nervous too, but unlike Charlie I had the advantage of a few hosepipes inside me instead of a broom handle and so was past caring. Princess Margaret turned to look at me. I'd never seen her this close before, although I had performed in front of her at another charity gig. Very majestic she was, too, wearing this heavy brocade gown all studded with stones. It must've weighed a ton. We shook hands, and I couldn't help noticing her eyes. Very piercing, they seemed to tell a story all of their own. A story of generations spent sitting on thoroughbred horses at the head of cavalry charges.

'Hello,' she said. 'How nice to see you again. Didn't you do a show for us at the Tower in aid of the Spastics in September 1974?'

I was dumbfounded. She actually remembered: though it did cross my mind that him in the hush puppies had probably clued her up before they left the palace. Never mind, I didn't care. This was great. If only Mum could see me now.

'By the way,' said Her Royal Highness as we came to the end of our pleasant little chat, 'where are the others in your group?'

'Oh, they're in the pub drinking hosepipes,' I replied.

HRH chose not to enquire further into this.

'I should meet them, you know.'

'Yes, ma'am,' I said. 'I'll go and get them.'

Like hell I will, I thought, as I made my way over to the free bar. They're all pissed out of their minds. She won't miss them.

But I'd reckoned without the acute hearing of the drenched lackey. Ten minutes and a couple of rums later I felt a tap on my shoulder.

'Excuse me,' he said. 'Would you come and intwoduce your gwoup to Her Woyal Highness now.'

I looked across at a large, bedraggled crowd, my group, in the middle of which could be seen a curly mop of hair. Newman's. Oh my God, no, I thought. I hope to Christ he's got his trousers on. I had visions of being hauled off to the Tower, my arms tied behind my back, head on the block and a short back and sides the hard way. I closed my eyes and prayed to God to make him go away. I opened them again and he was still there.

I followed the lackey towards the royal queue, my heart in my mouth. The whole saloon bar were there before me, including people I'd never seen before in my life. The idiot had rushed into the pub and shouted 'Joe Bwown's gwoup follow me,' whereupon everyone in the bar had done just that. Now here I was, with Princess Margaret looking enquiringly and patiently at me, while a complete load of strangers waited to be introduced. I took a deep breath and began.

'This is our bass player, Jeff Peters.'

'Hello,' said HRH. 'A very nice performance. Thank you.'

Jeff was moved along and Hynesy took his place. I stepped forward again.

'This is our drummer, Dave Hynes.'

'Hello. A very nice performance. Thank you.'

Next came someone I didn't know, a cloth cap on his head and a hand-rolled dog-end stuck to his upper lip. My head was beginning to swim.

'Our bassoon player,' I heard myself say, grabbing the cap from his head and stuffing it in his pocket. On and on it went, like a nightmare. I was running out of instruments. Now I knew why André Previn never introduced the London Symphony Orchestra. Finally the unavoidable moment came and there stood Newman. I knew the look on his face. It meant trouble. I lowered my eyes. At least he was wearing trousers.

'And who are you?' Princess Margaret asked him, beating me to it.

'I'm Tony Newman.'

'And where are you from, Mr Newman?'

There was a pause. Newman looked round to make sure he had everyone's attention.

An early 1980s publicity shot for 'The Ted Song' from the TV film Tribute to a Teddy Boy.

'I'm a clown from an ice-cream factory,' he shouted.

HRH wasn't having any. She looked straight through his eyes to the back of his head.

'I BEG YOUR PARDON,' she said icily.

Newman's face went ashen. He sobered up immediately. He didn't know what to say. Everyone waited. The whole foyer was stock-still. Then suddenly, in desperation, Newman dropped to one knee, tugged at his forelock and blurted out:

'W-W-Woodford Green, ma'am.'

The great Newman, king of the loons, reduced to jelly by one royal look.

Magic!

26 Mum and the loonie

One thing about living in the country, you get to meet all sorts. You do in town, come to that, but somehow they seem more eccentric in rural surroundings. Some, of course, are just plain stupid, like the people who move into a new 'country-style' estate in a nearby village and after a couple of weeks get up a petition because a local farmer's pigs stink. Or those who move into a pretty little 'des. res.' by the cricket ground and complain because they're always having to have the windows replaced. That's why, when I thought I'd try my hand at country squiring, I bought a place just down the road from a sort of open mental hospital. I knew I'd be among friends.

After all, with Mum living in a cottage on the edge of the orchard, I wasn't likely to worry too much about a few funny-looking blokes wandering round the woods and peeping in the windows. Except for their sakes of course, especially after what she'd done to the cat and these strange ideas she had about reincarnation.

The unusual thing about the cat was that it was ginger. Most of the cats in my mother's life – and there were quite a few – were like Mr Henry Ford's Model T. Any colour you like provided it's black. That way, she reckoned, it didn't matter whether they were dirty or clean. But this fellow was ginger, wild and a tom. She'd found him staring at her one morning when she was hanging out her woollen drawers in the garden and immediately set out to tame him. A bit of food and some milk attracted him closer to the cottage and it wasn't more than a couple of weeks before he was sitting in her lap by the fireside. No one else could get near the thing, but he'd let Mum do anything to him. He became her party piece – fair brought the house down, it did. She'd tuck its head under her arm, hold its legs so that it couldn't scratch her, and put its tail between her teeth, bite on it and march up and down the room like a Scottish piper with the cat screeching its head off like the bloody bagpipes. You never heard anything like it. You wouldn't want to.

But that wasn't the worst thing she did to it. The moment she had it tamed, she took it down to the vet's and had it neutered!

'I thought it was yer father come back,' she told me, 'an' I wasn't taking any chances.' Her voice went down an octave and she became confidential. 'I only 'ad it twice, yer know. Once was you and once was yer brother. An' I only did it then 'cause I felt sorry for 'im.'

I looked at the cat sleeping peacefully on her lap. Poor old Dad. First time round he lost his teeth. Second time . . . I couldn't see him coming back a third time.

So you can understand why, when strange-looking men were wandering about the place, I called the hospital pretty quickly to send the hurry-up wagon round to collect them. Which is what I'd have done this particular day – if only.

I was upstairs getting ready to go out when our cleaning lady shouted from the landing.

'Hey, Joe, there's one of them loony blokes mooching about your orchard eating apples.'

'Take no notice of him, love,' I shouted from the shower. 'He'll probably go away.'

''E don't 'alf look daft,' she said.

He must be, I thought. They're cooking apples. I turned off the shower and wrapped a towel around me, just in case she turned out to be one of those cleaning women who write their memoirs about famous people they've done for. But she'd gone back downstairs. Silence reigned, if you didn't count the cleaning lady's radio, the television, the vacuum cleaner and a VC 10 on a flightpath home to Heathrow (the Brown household in communion with nature). No sooner had I given myself a final rub-down, though, than she belted up the stairs screaming 'Quick! Quick! He's gone in your mum's cottage!'

Blimey, I thought, grabbing some jeans and a T-shirt. She's not going to like that. By this time of her life, Mum was a bit of a late riser. She didn't go to bed till five in the morning because she'd sit up all night to see the deer in the woods. (A bit of a nature lover was Mum: loved animals, hated people, especially insurance men.)

This is why when I got to Mum's she was still in bed, but already reaching for the pepper pot she kept by her bed to ward off prospective rapists. The bloke from up the road was in there all right, standing by her bed, holding on to the electric light with one hand, a large cooking apple tucked under his left arm, while in his other hand he was holding Mum's china teapot which he was waving happily about. His mouth was working overtime but no words were emerging.

Mum didn't have this problem.

'Oo the bleedin' 'ell are you?' she was demanding.

The poor bloke – I learnt later he was a mute – could only stand there waving the teapot and opening and closing his mouth. When I jerked my thumb towards the door, he went out as quiet as a mouse and wandered into the woods.

This, I told myself, is definitely not on. Helping himself to apples from the orchard, OK. But strange geezers standing over the beds of seventy-year-old widows is just not on. I decided to phone that hospital, get them to send someone down here, and when he came I'd give him a right bollocking. Then it occurred to me: at the rate our bloke was travelling, it must have taken him an hour at least to get from the hospital to us. So they must've known he was missing by this time. That really made me angry.

Instead I decided to call the police and say there's a strange bloke wandering about. *He* wouldn't get into trouble, but with any luck they'd get their knuckles rapped at the hospital. It might stop them being so careless with the people they're supposed to be looking after. For all I knew the woods might've been full of them.

Back at the house and thumbing through the phone book for the number of the local nick, I was getting more and more annoyed at what had happened. She might have thrown him through the window, and I'd have had to get a carpenter in to replace it. I'd only just had the place done up, too. And now I couldn't find the number I wanted. Sod this for a game of soldiers, I thought. I'll dial 999. Which I did.

'Emergency. Which service do you require?'

'Old Bill, please, love.'

'Bill's on nights this week. Do you want to speak to Trev?'

'Sorry, love. I meant the police.'

'Why didn't you say so then, wasting my time like that? I'll want to see those queens first, Trevor. Sorry, caller. Name, address and telephone number.'

I gave the details.

'Not *the* Joe Brown?'

'No. Just another one.'

'You'd think his manager would have made him change his name, wouldn't you.'

Come on, love. The bloke'll be in Wales by this time, poor sod.

'Are you getting me the police?' I asked with a note of desperation.

'Don't panic, Mr Brown. We'll have someone there before you can say knife.'

Down by the woods the cleaning lady was standing guard outside Mum's cottage. She brought the broom to attention and saluted as I approached.

'I bin watchin' 'im, Joe. 'E's acting very strange. After you'd gone to the phone 'e tried to get a drink out of that.'

She pointed to an old galvanized bucket, a relic from the Walton-on-the-Naze pub outing of 1948. It was full of dirty water and old floor cloths.

'It's bin standing there a fortnight, y'know, Joe.'

'I'll get Vicki to tell Mum not to bother with the housework. She's getting much too old for it.'

'I told 'er that meself but she threatened to set yer father on to me.'

'That won't do you any good, mate,' I said and walked round the house to wait for the police at the front gate. Twenty minutes later I was still standing there when the cleaning lady called out that the phone was ringing. I knew it was. I could hear it.

'Good afternoon, sir.' (Already, I thought, looking at my watch?) 'This is the police station. Where was it you said you lived?'

'Don't bother,' I said. 'He's gone now.'

'No, no, it's no bother. No bother at all. You just stay where you are. Where did you say you are?'

I gave him the address.

'Right. We'll have someone there before you can say Jack Robinson.'

I tried it.

'Jack Robinson.'

And still there was no sign of them. But somewhere in the distance I could hear a siren. Moments later there was a screech of tyres as round the corner came this big jam sandwich on two wheels, a big white motor with a red stripe along the side and a blue light spinning round the top. Up the drive it races, gravel flying everywhere, and broadsides to a halt. The door's flung open and out jumps this red-neck copper, slashed-peak cap set so low that he couldn't see properly without holding his head at a ninety-degree angle.

'Where is he? Where is he?' he demands, jangling a pair of handcuffs and looking at me menacingly. He obviously knows a mental case when he sees one.

'Hang on a minute, mate,' I coughed through the settling dust. 'He's only a poor old loony who's wandering about in the woods somewhere. He's not going to harm anybody.'

'I'll have him. I'll have him. I'll have the cuffs on him, just you see. Where are these woods?'

'Calm down. Please. Calm down. I don't know where he is exactly. That's why you're here. To find him.'

'I'll have him. I'll have him. Get in the car. Get in the car.'

I knew it was a waste of time arguing, so I got in the front seat. Or half in. I was still trying to get the other leg in when we were spinning round the drive and racing back out on to the main road like a rat from a drainpipe, siren going full bore and the blue light flashing as he hared off in search of our wayward loonie.

Ten minutes and a new gearbox later he's still going on about what he's going to do when he catches him. Like the gearbox, I'd had enough. I leant across and switched off the siren. I was getting hoarse from yelling above the noise. The car skidded to a halt to the accompaniment of burning rubber.

'I'll have you for that. I'll have you for that.'

'Look, mate.' I was using the voice the kids got when I was making one last attempt before my patience went. 'The bloke we're looking for, he's not a criminal. He's just a harmless bloke who wandered away from the mental hospital up the road. So why don't we just calm down and go up to the hospital and report him missing?'

'CALM DOWN! CALM DOWN! It's all right for you, living out here in the country. Do you know what I was doing for six years before they posted me here? Do you? Do you?'

I shook my head.

'I was a military policeman in Hong f------ Kong. Doing a man's job. Do you know what I've been doing since I came here?'

I shook my head again.

'Taking old ladies' dogs back to them, that's what. Now I get my first loonie and you're telling me to calm bloody down.'

He threw the Rover into first gear, let out the clutch, set the siren alight and was touching eighty by the time we hurtled through the hospital gates. We were going only marginally slower when we hit the first speed ramp, bounced four feet in the air and landed with a thump that shook my teeth and added the suspension to the gearbox as candidates for replacement. The grounds were full of people mooching about, one bloke planting plastic flowers in a border while his mate went along after him watering them. Neither of them batted an eyelid at our entrance. They probably thought it was normal.

In we went through the big front doors, me striding out manfully to keep up with the copper as he double-marched down the tiled corridor, his regulation boots sending little sparks flying in all directions. Johnny the Genie had nothing on him when it came to pyrotechnics. Straight to the warden's office, where our man slid smartly to attention in front of the desk and saluted.

'What seems to be the trouble, boys?' asked the warden in a gentle Welsh voice.

'Reported missing, one loonie. Sir!' barked the copper, his military training apparent in the presence of authority. 'And we're after him.' He waved the handcuffs in the warden's face.

'Now, now, I'm sure there's no need for those. Let's be calm about this now.'

'Don't tell him that,' I said quickly as the copper's face turned purple. 'He used to be a military policeman in Singapore.'

'Hong f------ Kong,' he screamed, and began muttering something about the good old days and seventeen murders a week. I left him to it and turned to explain the situation to the warden. I must admit that I was somewhat taken aback by his nonchalant attitude. He didn't look in the least concerned: just sat moving his fountain pen about the desk as if playing a one-piece game of chess. Trust me to get one who's a Welsh do-gooder.

'Ah yes, that must be Malcolm, that is. I wouldn't worry, you know. He's always getting out, Malcolm is. Do you know, we have to strap him up at night with a board across his shoulders to stop him climbing up and jumping off the roof.' He chuckled merrily. 'Oh yes, he's a bit of a lad, our Malcolm is.'

But if I was taken aback, the copper was fuming. He couldn't believe what the Welsh warden was saying.

'Doesn't it strike you as a bit dodgy,' I asked, 'him standing over an old lady's bed, clutching the electric light bulb and waving her own teapot at her?'

'Do, do, do! There's no harm in it. No harm at all.'

'No harm in it? My mum's over seventy.'

'That's right,' joined in the copper. 'She could've had a heart attack.'

This compassionate side to his nature took me by surprise.

'I wasn't thinking of her,' I told them. 'I was worried about *him.* If she'd have got out of bed she'd have bloody well killed him.'

The copper's face lit up at the thought of a possible homicide and the phone rang. Malcolm had been found. Indeed captured. The poor sod had been locked in a garage. So off we went again in the jam sandwich.

No lights flashing this time. No siren. Very low key. There wasn't even any need for the handcuffs, ruefully rattled by the copper as Malcolm walked gently off to the hurry-up wagon which had followed us.

'I'm very very sorry you've been troubled,' said the Welsh warden to the lady of the house.

'Oh, that's all right,' she said graciously. 'I think the poor chap was thirsty. That's why he came here. He was drinking the water from the dog's bowl.'

Poor bloke. I felt sorry for him. First that foul stuff in Mum's bucket and then the dog's water.

'So I gave him a glass of milk and a biscuit.'

Well, at that the Welshman went mad.

'You did what?'

The woman stepped back nervously.

'I . . . I gave him a glass of milk and a biscuit.'

'You shouldn't have done that,' he screamed. 'He'll keep coming back.'

'Calm down, sir,' said the copper, looking hopefully at his handcuffs. 'Just calm down now.'

I left them to it and walked home through the woods. I didn't see any loonies but I wouldn't have been surprised. It seemed the sanest place to be just then.

27 A fair cop, guv'nor, and no mistake

Coppers and cars: a dangerous combination in my book. If they tell me I'm speeding, there's no way I'm going to disagree with them. I mean, they've got the law on their side, haven't they?

'Awfully sorry, mate,' is what I usually say. 'I didn't see you parked there in that lady's drive with your radar trap. If I'd spotted you I'd have slowed down straight away.'

That way they know you're on the level: that you're not taking the mickey out of them. In my case it helps that they've probably seen me on telly, because they'll have a chat and send me off with a warning.

'Never guess who I pulled in today?' he'll say to the wife and kids at supper that night.

'No, dear,' his wife will say automatically and his kids' heads won't even move from the television set.

'Joe Brown,' he'll say.

'Oh,' says his wife and gives him another spoonful of instant mashed potato for good measure.

Buddy Holly had a good line with policemen who stopped him for speeding.

'Look, man, what is this? Here am I, racing to get to this concert on time to help promote the great state of Texas and all you can think about is stopping me for speeding. Where's your pride in the state, man?'

Or words to that effect. Then there was the Hollywood film star – James Dean or one of that lot – who always tucked a century note into his driving licence. I'd never do that. For one thing, you can't always trust a copper to give you the correct change. Usually I'm lucky, but every so often the luck doesn't hold and I'm left to my own devices.

One night Vicki and I were stopped on our way out of London. The copper obviously recognized me, I could tell that from his first reaction, yet just as obviously he didn't like me. I was getting the same vibes I used to get walking off the pier at Yarmouth.

'This your vehicle?' he starts off.

'Yes, officer.' Nothing smart. Just keep it simple.

'Let me see your licence.'

I handed it over.

'What's the matter, officer?'

'I'll ask the questions.'

Oh dear. One of those. He wrote some details in his notebook.

'What's your registration, Mr Brown?'

'What's my registration?' I asked.

'Yes. The car number.'

I shook my head and looked blank: an easy trick once you get the hang of it.

'I don't know.'

'How long have you had the car?'

'Years.' I suppose it had a number plate.

'But you don't know the number. Don't expect me to believe that, do you? Where'd you get it then?'

I'm in for it here, I thought.

'Look, officer, if I was speeding, I'm sorry. I'm running late and I'm in a hurry, I've got a clean licence, and if you're going to nick me, do me a favour and nick me quick 'cause I'm really in a rush.'

I could hear the edge creeping into my voice.

'Not so fast,' he said and began walking round the car, checking the tyres and the lights: the whole do-it-by-the-book bit. He knows he's holding me up, and he knows I'm getting more and more angry by the minute, plenty of which are ticking away. Eventually he finishes his round.

'Now listen,' I said. 'Don't think this is going to stop here. I'm going to take this to court and contest it. I know lawyers as well, you know' – getting on my high horse – 'and I'm going to make a case of this.'

'You may do as you will, Mr Brown. I'm still going to charge you with speeding, and you had better have your documents at a police station in twenty-four hours or the charge will be more than just speeding.'

He flipped open his notebook and this terrible thought went through my mind.

'Are you going to caution me?'

'It's not essential.'

'So I could call you a jumped-up little Caesar hiding behind a uniform and you wouldn't use it against me.'

'I might.'

'But you didn't write it down in your book. Did he, Vick?'

Vicki shook her head. The copper made as if he was going to write.

'If you're going to put that down, you can write this first. Ready? "It's a fair cop, guv'nor, and no mistake." '

There was a long silence.

'You haven't written it down yet.'

'You can't say that.'

'I just have. You've got to write it down. It's evidence.'

He snapped his notebook shut.

'If you think I'm standing up in court and saying that, you've got another think coming. Go on. Piss off!'

So I got away with it. You can just imagine the scene, can't you.

'Did the accused say anything when you cautioned him, officer?'

'Er, um, well, yes sir.'

'And what did he say, officer?'

Opens notebook and reads.

'It's a fair cop, guv'nor, and no mistake.'

No way.

It doesn't always work out like that though. Another time, driving my Austin Healey, I was going through Manchester to Granada Studios, doing forty-five in a thirty mile-an-hour zone, when this copper appeared alongside me on a motorbike and waved me down. I stopped, he pulled up in front of me, and I sat in the car as he got off the bike and walked over.

'In a little bit of a hurry, aren't . . .' and suddenly he recognized me. 'Blow me, if it isn't Joe Brown.'

'That's right.' Big grin.

'What d'you know! I watch you on the telly. Think you're marvellous. Kids too. They think the world of you. And my missus.'

'That's great. I'm sorry about the speeding. I'm supposed to be in the studio in half an hour.'

'Do us a favour, will you, Joe? An autograph for the kids.'

He pulled his pen and notebook from a pocket.

'Hang on,' I said, 'I've got a photograph here somewhere.' I looked in my bag for some of the publicity handouts the Granada PR department had given me the day before. 'Better still,' I said, remembering, 'I've got some big ones in the boot.'

'If you could make it to Jane and Jennie,' he said as I removed the spare wheel and a couple of suitcases in search of the packet of photos.

So I wrote 'To Jane and Jennie. All the best. Joe Brown.'

The copper undid his tunic, put the photo against his chest, and did up his tunic, looking as pleased as Punch.

'That's terrific of you, lad. Terrific. You've no idea how thrilled they'll be. Now then, let's have a look at your licence.'

Whereupon he booked me. Just like that! I had to laugh. And I bet he did too when he got back to the station and told his mates how he'd done me. The funny thing was, even when I was fined I didn't mind one little bit.

28 Circus star

It must be every kid's dream to be asked to join in the circus. I wasn't a kid at the time, only at heart, but there was no way I was going to say no when Billy Smart came up one night and offered me the star role in the finale. Besides, the circus is in my blood. My mum's father was a trick rider with Buffalo Bill's Wild West Show and then worked with circuses in England: her mum's people were circus folk too. I've got sawdust in my veins – as well as in my head.

Every year Billy Smart's Circus did a grand charity night on the common at Blackheath. It was well patronized by a lot of show business people and Billy and his family were very kind to us: plenty of champagne and good seats for ourselves and our families so we could watch the show in comfort. We didn't have to perform: simply had to be there and give our support.

This particular year, Billy came up to me during the interval, asked if we were enjoying ourselves and whether or not I'd seen that year's production. No, I said. What's so different?

'The finale's great,' he replied. 'It's the Seventh Cavalry. We've got loads of Red Indians and this pretty bird with long blonde hair. The Indians capture the girl, tie her up to the totem pole and are just about to give her the chop when in comes the Seventh Cavalry and rescues her.'

'Sounds great.'

Just then the band struck up for the opening of the second half and Billy left us. Ten minutes later, however, he was back.

'Listen, Joe. I've just had a thought. You ride, don't you?'

'I can stay on a horse, yes.'

'Well, how'd you like to lead the charge in the finale?'

Following in the footsteps of my grandfather, who was a star rider in Buffalo Bill's Wild West Show.

By this time I'd had a few glasses of champagne and was game for anything.

'Not half,' I told him. 'What do I have to do?'

'It's a piece of cake,' said Billy, sitting down next to me. 'You know that big grey stallion you rode when we did the publicity shots for the *Daily Mirror* a few years ago?'

I nodded.

'We'll put you on him. All you've got to do is gallop him four or five times round the outer ring, then turn into the inner ring and rescue the girl. That's the end of the show. Easy, isn't it.'

'I can't wait.'

'Right. You sit here and watch the show for a while. I'll go and sort you out a uniform and some guns and tell the ring hands what's happening.'

Off he went, and a while later one of his girls came to say it was time for me to go out and get changed. Billy was in his caravan with this real cavalry officer's uniform. None of your usual circus tat but proper cloth and beautifully tailored. It felt terrific to wear, and when I looked at myself in the mirror I could just see myself chasing Apaches up and down the Panhandle until John Ford shouted 'Cut!' Except that there was something missing.

'Where are my guns?'

'Not yet,' said Billy.

'Why not?' I demanded. I was feeling undressed without them.

'They're real guns. Joe. You'll be firing blanks, of course, but they're still real guns and there are lots of restrictions, same as in the theatre. You'll get them just before you go on, and you'll have to sign for them.'

'Oh, that's all right. I understand.'

Which I did, though every now and then I couldn't resist giving him a small reminder. We had another glass of champagne and then he took me out to renew acquaintances with the horse. A lovely fellow he was: big and powerful but with a very light touch. Riding him would be no problem: it was a matter of sitting on his back and off he'd go. The rest of the Seventh Cavalry were already mounted up and ready to ride, so I was pretty conscious of trying to make a good impression. I swung up into the saddle and waited, as two of the ring hands adjusted the stirrups and girth strap.

'OK, all comfortable up here, Billy. Now, where's me guns, sheriff?' I demanded for the nth time.

'Just a minute. Are you sure you know what you're supposed to do?'

'Of course. Just give me the guns.'

However, he still went through the whole routine. Galloping round four or five times, into the inner ring, shoot a few Indians who'll fall down dead, rescue the bird.

'Don't worry about the horse, Joe. The horse knows what's happening anyway.'

'Fine. Where're my guns?'

'Give him his guns,' Billy said resignedly. One of the ring hands held up a box containing two marvellous Navy Colts – the genuine article – which I then had to sign for. I slipped them into the holsters and now I was ready. The big moment was approaching.

'Right?' asked Billy. 'Off you go.'

We shot into the big top at a gallop and raced round the outer ring with a thunder of hooves and the trumpeter blowing da-da da-da da-da da-da behind me. None of your musical cornet-playing cavalry charge music you get in the pictures. Just a lot of staccato blasts as the trumpeter was jolted up and down with his horse. Not that the audience minded –

they thought it was great. The kids were all on their feet shouting and cheering as we raced round and round. I almost forgot we were supposed to go in and shoot some Indians, but fortunately the horse remembered his lines. Suddenly we were doing a sharpish right turn into the inner ring – or at least the horse was. I tried to bring myself round with him and ended up flying straight over his head. The kids were not impressed. I got more boos than a pantomime villain.

However, I still had hold of the horse and, showman to the last, I clutched my chest as if I'd been shot and staggered out of the big top, dragging the horse behind me. He must've wondered what the hell was going on. This wasn't part of his script.

When we got outside, I noticed that the saddle had slipped right under his belly, which was a bit odd, to say the least. I lifted up the stirrup flap to look at the strap and found that, while it was still fastened, the buckle was about four rings down from where it should've been. There was a big black mark on the strap where the buckle usually went, and I knew enough about horses and circus people to be sure that this wasn't any old saddle for any old horse. This particular saddle was meant for this particular horse. Someone had set that buckle loose on purpose. I'd been done! And when I saw a couple of sniggering ring hands in the yard, I reckoned I knew who by.

OK, I thought, I'll show the bastards. I tightened the girth again and swung back up into the saddle. Wild Joe Brown wasn't going to be outdone. I gripped the reins between my teeth, drew the Navy pieces and kicked the palomino back into the ring at full gallop, firing shots as I went. Thunderous, they were, and when I'd loosed off both cylinders I realized how deathly quiet it was. I'd deafened myself. Then gradually my hearing returned and I could hear the strains of people singing 'Send her victorious, happy and . . .' I looked around: everyone, audience and performers alike, was standing to attention. Well, not the cavalry. They were sitting to attention. And all the dead Indians were on their feet again, standing there with their feathers upright, except for the chief who was standing with his headdress under his arm, so revealing a great white band on his forehead where the warpaint stopped and the headdress had started.

It dawned on me. The show was over. They were singing 'God Save The Queen' and the show was over. The full impact struck me. There they were, all standing to attention singing the national anthem, when this lunatic had come thundering in on a big grey horse firing off his guns like some cowboy in a B-movie. No wonder I haven't been asked back since.

29 Funny thing about funerals

I don't know what it is about funerals. They're obviously very sad occasions, yet when you hear people talking about them it's always the funny side that comes to the fore. I don't know that I've ever heard a sad story about a funeral.

My mum hated them. I remember once when a very old friend, a woman who'd been like a mother to my mum, died. Mum was very cut up about it.

'Mrs Thatcher's dead,' she said to me when I popped in to see her.

'Oh dear, I am sorry. When's the funeral?'

'Don't know,' replied Mum.

'You are going, aren't you?'

'No thanks,' said Mum. 'Anyway it's too far.'

'Where is it then?'

'Don't know.'

'How do you know it's too far then?' I asked.

'It must be,' she said. 'She lived in Maidstone and that's miles away.'

'It's not that far,' I told her. 'I'll take you.'

'No you won't. Besides, I'm not going.'

'But you've got to. They'll be expecting you to.'

'Mrs Thatcher won't,' said Mum, and you couldn't deny her logic. 'She knows I never liked funerals.'

'Come on, Mum, you've got to go. Mrs Thatcher was like a mother to you. You've told me so yourself.'

'Look,' she said. 'I ain't goin' and that's final. I 'ate funerals. The only funeral I'm ever goin' to is me own, and I'm not bothered about goin' to that one – yet.'

'What about mine?' I joked. 'You'll come to that, won't you?'

'No I won't. They 'ad to drag me to your father's. And then I nearly fell down the bleedin' 'ole.'

So much for Mum's outlook on funerals. But there are people who wouldn't miss one for the world. They revel in them, it seems. Just think how many times you've enquired of someone – 'Have you seen old so and so about?' – only to be told: 'The last time I saw him was at the funeral.' Whether it's out of respect, or just a morbid fascination with death, I wouldn't know. But if someone in the neighbourhood dies, you can bet your boots old so-and-so will be at the funeral. Perhaps he or she's trying to ensure a good turnout at his or her own – or maybe old so-and-so has a secret passion for ham sandwiches with the crusts cut off? Who knows.

When Vicki's Gran died, the whole family had to go to the funeral: and when I say *had*, I mean had. The old boy would never have forgiven anyone who didn't turn up. Not only that, we all had to go to Liverpool to see him *before* the funeral just so that we could pay our respects and find out if there was anything special required of us on the mournful day.

Grandad Thompson, an old First World War veteran, was the undisputed head of the family: a small bloke, about five foot seven, quite slim and very dapper. His nose was his most outstanding feature – literally. He had three brothers and four sisters and they all looked the same. There was Our Eva, Our Esther, Our Nellie, Our May, Our Alec, Our Sammy and Our Billy, the rich one. Whenever a baby was born into the family, they'd all stand around the pram and the greatest compliment they felt they could pay was 'Oh, he's a Thompson all right. He's got the Thompson nose.' I always felt sorry for the kid, looking up at all those noses and wondering if one day he'd have one just like that of his very own. Some of them did, and they also inherited certain other characteristics, such as the Thompson height. This was to prove to be an important factor at the funeral, because at the time of Granny's funeral, most of Grandad's generation of Thompsons had gone to meet the great nostril in the sky.

Three days before the funeral, Vicki and I drove up to Liverpool to see Grandad. We stayed with Vicki's sister Mary and her husband Neil, who, not to beat about the bush, wasn't too fond of the old boy. I can't say that I blame him: Grandad Thompson could be very awkward at times. And as Neil has a *different*-shaped nose, he has often fallen foul of the Thompsons. At the same time, I think he always respected the old man.

Apart from his *different*-shaped nose, Neil was also blessed with a cutting and usually wicked sense of humour. On the day when we had to go and see Grandad, Neil decided that he and Mary would come with us. We arrived at the house to find nearly all the family there. Thompsons mostly. You could pick them by their noses. They'd all congregated in the front room, with the old man sitting on a chair at one end, holding court. No one could dispute how deeply he had felt his loss. The poor old fellow looked pale and thin and sad in his eyes. All the family were standing about in complete silence. Vicki and Mary went over and offered their condolences while I, never knowing what to say in these circumstances, gave a little wave from where I was standing.

Neil, the bastard, saluted!

Grandad, acknowledging our greetings, said, 'We're just about to discuss the funeral arrangements.' And began: 'Our Eva and Our May, you'll make the sarnies?'

'OK, Bob,' came the honoured reply.

'Our Eric, you'll officiate with the cars. Our Billy, you'll look after the flowers. Our Cyril, you'll stay here and look after the telly.' So it went on until he came to the thing that was undoubtedly the most important to him.

'As to the coffin bearers.' Everybody fell silent. He paused for quite some time. 'Our Charlie, you'll take the bottom left-hand corner.'

'Thanks, Bob.'

'Our Tommy, bottom right hand.'

Somebody at the back coughed.

'Oh yes,' said Grandad. 'Sidney. Top left.'

Sidney smiled proudly.

'Now. Who have we left out?'

A sea of arms shot ceilingwards. 'Me! Me!' called someone.

Grandad looked slowly round the room.

'Harry,' he said and a spontaneous round of applause broke out. Now, was it going to be four or six? Everyone held his breath. Suddenly Grandad looked straight at Neil and asked in a very quiet voice: 'Neil? Will you do it?'

Neil was a bit taken aback but he nodded.

'Aye. All right.'

Then without warning he turned to me and asked, 'And you?'

'I'd be proud to, Grandad,' I said.

As we were leaving the house, Neil sidled up to me.

'Er, you finally made the big time then.'

'What do you mean?'

'You know. Carryin' the coffin.'

I could tell this was a wind-up.

'Don't start,' I said. 'All I need is you sniggering alongside me at the funeral and we'll drop the bloody thing.'

'Did you notice anything funny with the coffin bearer arrangements?' he asked.

I shook my head.

'Look at me.'

I looked.

'So?' I asked.

'I'm five foot seven, right?'

'Right,' I nodded.

'How tall are the Thompsons?'

'About five foot seven,' I replied.

'Right. And how tall are you?'

It hit me.

'I'm six foot one.'

'Exactly,' said Neil. 'You're going to look a right berk, aren't you, with the coffin on your shoulder while the rest of us have to balance it on our heads.'

'Oh hell,' I said. 'I never thought of that.'

'I did,' said Neil, grinning evilly.

The next two days before the funeral were murder, what with Vicki and Mary in tears for much of the time and Neil waltzing round the house singing 'Tote dat barge, Lift dat bale.' Very funny. Luckily the embarrassment wasn't to be. Somebody must've pointed out the problem to Grandad and I was excused from duty. Not without some regret, I might add. I'd genuinely considered it an honour to be asked.

The funeral itself was a very sad affair. Even Neil was upset. The old man himself looked suddenly very lonely, old and unsure of himself.

Afterwards I got talking to some people, with the result that when I came to go, everyone had left for the house except two of the aunties who'd been left standing on the pavement because no one wanted to sit in a car with them. The last of Our Eric's cars drew up to the kerb. I opened the door for the ladies: one climbed in all right, but the other one was a bit slow so I nipped in myself to give her a hand. Consequently when we were all aboard I found myself sitting between the two of them. The journey itself was only a mile and a half or thereabouts, but for the first mile neither of them said a word. Then they started.

First Aunty: 'Mary, Mary. Our poor Mary.'

Second Aunty: 'One of de finest people God ever put breath into.'

First Aunty: 'I know.'
Second Aunty: 'Oh God.'
First Aunty: 'Didn't the mortician do a lovely job?'
Second Aunty: 'She looked beautiful.'
First Aunty: 'Aye. But you know I think that week in New Brighton did her good.'

And so it went on until, by the time we reached the house, it was,
First Aunty: 'She never did pay me for that wool I sent her, you know.'
Second Aunty: 'I wonder what happened to that gold watch of Our Alec's?'

When we went in the house, everything was much the same as it had been on the previous occasion. Grandad was sitting in the same chair, with all the family standing round, apart from detachments of aunties scuttling about distributing crustless ham sandwiches and endless cups of tea. From the clusters of menfolk could be heard the occasional low murmurings. 'They should never have dropped Dalglish.' 'Clemence. Our Ray. Magic.' 'Not the same at the back since Tommy Smith left.' Grandad sat there looking lost.

The door burst open and in came Uncle Charlie, the life and soul of any party.

'Well well, well well, well,' he began. 'I'm sure Our Mary wouldn't like to see so many unhappy faces. How about a song?'

Everybody ignored him. But Charlie wasn't to be outdone.

'Did you hear the one about the Catholic priest and the nymphomaniac? You'll die laughing.'

Everybody shuddered. Charlie got the message and lapsed into an uneasy, uncharacteristic silence. It was too much for him though, and spotting Vicki he shouted across the room, still trying to instil some party spirit into the gathering.

'Hey dere, Our Vicki. D'you know when you're on the telly wit de Breakaways, are you the one in the middle?'

Vicki nodded.

'I thought so,' said Charlie. 'I recognize you by your watch strap.'

30 Brown's Home Brew

'It's a pity that Joe Brown seems to be out of the British rock scene – three years back [1974] *he was leading one of the country's most exciting bands, Brown's Home Brew. The band's album 'Together' consisted of raw, earthy rock at its very best, influenced by a number of musical styles including country, gospel and folk.*

'Brown's Home Brew comprised Joe himself on guitar and vocals, his wife Vicki (also vocals), Joe Fagin (bass, vocals), David Hynes (drums, vocals), Roger McKew (guitar) and Tony Williams (keyboards, vocals). They are six of the most talented performers on the scene – but unfortunately it was a band little heard.'

Coming across old press cuttings like that can make you sad, it can make you mad. It's like a review I once read of the album 'Together'. After being very enthusiastic about the band and the songs, the reviewer ended on a note of caution: 'Joe knows the direction he wants his music to travel in. The big question is whether his public will let him travel away from his past.' The answer to that was no, they wouldn't.

Two people encouraged my interest in country rock: first and foremost, Dave Hynes, and then Roger Cook. Of gentle disposition for a drummer and with a definite artistic streak, Dave was by far the biggest influence. We got together originally to record a Crosby, Stills and Nash song called 'Helplessly Hoping'. It was my introduction to close-harmony singing and poetic lyrics and I was immediately hooked, much to the disappointment of my manager, who was dead against long hair, hippies and flower power. He could see his spiky-haired cheeky chappy slipping away from him – and a good income going with him.

The way I saw it, I was at a stage in my life when I needed to expand musically. Though only in my early thirties, I'd done a West End musical, royal variety shows, several films, TV shows, had hit records, played top night spots and cabarets around the country, and been in countless pantomimes – not to mention numerous rock and roll tours. (That's my trouble. Given half a chance I'll turn my hand to anything.) With all that behind me, I didn't think it unreasonable that I should be allowed to do something I'd set my heart on. George Cooper, on the other hand, couldn't understand it. He thought I was throwing my career away on a five-minute wonder. He may have been right, but from where I stood I think he missed the point entirely. To be good at anything you have to give it a try.

If Dave was the enthusiast, Roger Cook was the instigator. He was appearing with his group, Blue Mink, on a television show I'd also been asked to do. Usual old thing: the producer wanted me to do a comedy number, but this time I agreed only on the condition I could do a

I learned to play the fiddle in less than a week for Brown's Home Brew.

country rock song – 'The Yukon Railroad' – which the band and I had heard and liked. He agreed, so we set about arranging it to suit us.

'What'd sound really good would be a fiddle,' said Dave when we were rehearsing. Just the sort of bright suggestion I'd expect from a drummer. For a start we didn't have a fiddle. And even if we did, no one could play it. However, I remembered buying one years earlier from a bloke in Plaistow. Hadn't I lent it to my cousin Jim? Luckily he still had it, so that was problem number one solved.

Problem number two was learning to play it in less than a week. I thought about it: the violin is tuned in fifths – E, A, D, G – so I figured that as long as we played the song in the right key I might just about manage it. The first rehearsal was a scream. I was so terrible that Dave was in hysterics, and when Dave laughs at a funny situation you wonder if he's going to choke himself to death.

'It sounds like a cow wiv its tits caught in a mangle,' he said. 'I'll tell you what, Joe. Just keep smiling at the camera and they won't know the difference. If you get in real trouble, you can look at the guitarist as if it's his fault.'

Good advice that. I've been doing it ever since. Trouble is I'm often the guitarist and I'm sick of looking at my own mug.

By the time we recorded the TV show, I was good enough for us to get away with it. Not only that, after the show Roger Cook came up to me and said, 'That's the sort of music you should be doing. Get some of your own material together and I'll produce an album with you.'

He's pissed, I thought, and forgot about it. A week later he was on the phone.

'How are you getting on with it?'

'With what?'

'Writing that country rock stuff we talked about.'

Suddenly this was serious. Kind words over a few jars are one thing. Being chased along by a bloke like Roger Cook, who as well as being successful with Blue Mink was also an outstanding song-writer and producer, was a great compliment. Something had to be done about it.

'Come up and talk to Roger and me about it,' he suggested. Roger was his partner, Roger Greenaway, my old shooting partner from way back and now an important music publisher.

'I'll do that,' I said. After all, if those two didn't know what they were doing, who did? And I'd always liked country music. Good country music: not the 'D.I.V.O.R.C.E.' 'Stand By Your Man' sentimental stuff but the strong raunchy sound with good musicians playing slide and fiddle and dobro. I thought Roger Cook summed up the first kind that afternoon we met when he told me he was going to write the biggest country and western hit ever.

'I hope it's got a catchy middle eight,' I said.

'To hell with the tune,' he replied. 'The title alone will take it to number one.'

'What's it going to be called then?'

'"When I Visit Her Grave on Fridays, Even the Flowers Cry."'

I knew what he meant. I wasn't going to write songs like that. (Nor was Roger, I hasten to add.)

That year I was booked to do a summer season in Brighton, and during our spare time Dave and I set about writing some original material for the first Home Brew album. We'd take a couple of acoustic guitars up on to the Sussex Downs, find a nice quiet spot, pick out some tunes, drink some beer and talk. I'd tell him stories about my mum; he'd tell me stories about his wife ('When they say deuce at a tennis match she thinks that's when they go off for their barley water') and his dad, who according to Dave was a cat burglar (among other things), known in the trade as Flannelfoot.

Apparently he went down to the pub one Sunday lunchtime and didn't come back for seventeen years.

'Bring me back ten Woodbines,' Dave's mum shouted after him as he went down the street. 'And don't be late!'

How many times have you sat in the pub, listening to the locals bemoaning their fate and saying how they'd love to piss off somewhere? Dave's dad didn't moan about it. He went ahead and did it. Then he had the cheek to turn up on the doorstep seventeen years later, saying 'Hello, love. I couldn't get you Woodbines. Will Senior Service do?'

'I suppose so,' she replied ungratefully. 'And yer dinner's burnt.'

Then there was the time, according to Dave, when the old man, who'd been going straight for years, was persuaded by some young villains to help them do over a supermarket. It was coming up to Christmas and they thought they'd relieve the place of its stock of turkeys and chickens. They wanted Dave's dad to pick the lock. No problem at all to an old pro, and in return he got a share of the booty. Thirty-five frozen chickens and twenty-eight frozen turkeys.

'We was still defrosting the buggers when the Old Bill came round, saw 'em stacked up in the front room and booked 'im for receiving. Me mum was furious. She'd invited all the neighbours in for Christmas dinner.

'Anyway,' Dave continued, 'when he came up before the bench, the judge recognized him as one of his old customers.

The first Brown's Home Brew.

' "Mr Hynes," says his Lordship. "Of all the people I never expected to see before me again, it has to be you. I'm ashamed of you. What have you got to say for yourself?"

' "Well, Your Honour, it's like this, see. I'm an old-age pensioner and me doctor told me I should eat only white meat."

'Lucky old bugger got away with a caution,' concluded Dave. And we wrote another song. For all his stories, Dave was great to write with, always encouraging and full of enthusiasm. In no time at all, it seemed, we came up with a dozen good songs, and when we played them to Roger he was really excited and booked studio time straight away.

The original idea was that the Brown's Home Brew material should be geared towards the American market, and I still think that if we'd kept to that plan the band would have worked. We secured an attractive contract with Phonogram Records, one of whose executives was very keen on the project, and I sank my savings into setting up the band with all the right equipment, PA systems, lights and a road crew. I even changed my image by growing a beard and letting my hair grow.

The intention was to do the college circuit and gigs where no one had heard of Joe Brown, the Cockney chappy, but wanted to hear the band and its kind of music. It worked if the gig was right. I'd begin with some real lively fiddle, then the band would come in and we'd go from the opening instrumental straight into our first song, a fast, heavy number, follow it up with a slow song, then do another fast one. And stop. In front of an appreciative college crowd there'd be what seemed half a minute of silence – and then they'd erupt. Stamping, clapping, whistling. They loved it. The songs, the musicianship, Vicki's singing and Joe Fagin's growling voice on the heavier songs.

But that was the college circuit. There'd also be nights when we'd arrive at a gig to find the agent or the promoter had stuck up posters everywhere advertising Joe Brown and His Bruvvers. We'd begin with the Home Brew routine, but you could tell halfway through the opening set that this wasn't what they'd come to see. They wanted the Joe Brown they remembered from their teenage days: the Joe Brown they'd seen on telly. Not some hairy raising a storm with a bunch of ace musicians.

In the end I couldn't keep it going. Whereas Joe Brown could go out doing gigs and cabaret for £1,000 minimum a night, Brown's Home Brew was getting £150 for a gig that was costing me £400 to put on. By the time I called it a day I'd gone through the best part of £30,000. The album, despite good reviews, got little air-play and died a death. Yet that music is popular, especially today. Maybe 1974 was too early for it in Britain. Eleven years later I was performing country songs in front of packed houses in the West End in *Pump Boys and Dinettes*. And large crowds pack Wembley, Peterborough and other country music festivals.

Though there are country music festivals and country music festivals. Some are gigs put on by amateurs with good intentions at race courses and show grounds. Like the one I did in the north of England one Sunday while I was working in *Pump Boys*. Three hundred miles there and three hundred miles back in one day. It wasn't even that I needed the work, but the booking had been made some months earlier, and having said I'd do it, I didn't want to pull out. The stupid thing is that I knew I'd end up out of pocket long before I left home.

For a start I had to get a band together. In this instance I decided to use some of the lads from *Pump Boys*: Chad Stewart, for example, of Chad and Jeremy. That meant rehearsals of my stage act, and rehearsal studios in London cost £150 a day. Taking into account what I'd have to pay the band, I could count on the gig costing me at least £900.

There's something about a badly organized gig. The closer you get to it, the more you feel in your bones that it's going to go wrong. Then you arrive at the venue to be met by this guy who's been working all night trying to organize the show and you know he hasn't a clue what it's all about. You can't tell him, of course. He's convinced he knows it all, and as you stand there listening to all his problems, your heart sinks deeper down into your cowboy boots.

For a start, nothing's been done about the equipment that the contract specifically says will be supplied by the organizer. Guitars and back-line equipment we've brought with us in the cars, but not the sort of PA you'd provide yourself if you're on the road and travelling with a van. So now, because I care and because people have paid good money to come to see me, I rush about and sort it out myself as best I can. There's no other way – except to get back in the car and go home. And that only rebounds on you. I'd never put it past a promoter to get up on the stage and say 'That's Joe Brown for you, folks. Doesn't think we're good enough for him up here.'

At least the set went down well, and playing in front of a friendly audience just about wiped away the aggro that went beforehand. Until I asked the promoter for my money. 'That's the agent's affair,' he said. And I knew I'd be wasting my time because I'd already seen the agent – greasy trilby, striped shirt with spotted tie, down-at-heel shoes, more like a racecourse villain than an agent.

'I'm sorry, Joe, but there's nothing here now. You know the way it is. I've had to pay the other acts, and to be honest with you, Joe, that organizer's made a real pig's arse of the whole thing. If I'd known it was going to be like this, I'd never have booked you for it, I can promise you that, Joe. You know that, Joe.'

Oh yes, I know it all right. I've been here before. But what really gets me is that this bloke, and others like him, actually believes what he's telling me. In some ways that makes him more dangerous than the out-and-out villain. With this guy you could slip on his bullshit and break a leg. Yet I stood there and listened to all his so-called legitimate excuses. If the roles had been reversed and it was me telling him a load of cobblers, he'd probably have clocked me one and gone on his way.

'I'll send a cheque to your manager this week, Joe. I promise.'

Now I know I'll never get paid. There's nothing else to do but pack up the car and drive home. Next night I'm back on stage in the West End and laughing about it with Chad and the lads in the bar afterwards. But one morning during the week I'll wake up and I'll have stopped seeing the funny side of it. I'll just be pissed off with the world and angry that after years and years in this business there are still people ripping off and still people getting ripped off.

31 The galloping Major

One thing about living where I do now, I don't have to worry about the neighbours. There's a very nice couple who used to live in our farmhouse and have moved into the converted barn; and there's a horse in the paddock across the road. And that's it, mate. Every hour or so a Land-Rover comes past, and one day there were three lorries and a pick-up from the local council. People came from miles around just to see what a traffic jam looked like. I said to Vicki we could have put up some tables and chairs on the lawn and started doing teas.

It all seems a long way from the East End, and I wonder sometimes if I've been running away from it. But I don't think so. It would be impossible living in a neighbourhood where everyone knows you and wants to talk to you. I mean, you wouldn't be able to go down the garden to the bog without the neighbours running up asking for your autograph. Well, maybe not in the East End. They know how to bring you down to earth there, which is why I keep going back from time to time, just to keep my feet on the ground.

The first 'pop-star mansion' (as the papers put it) which I moved into was in Chigwell in east London. It was countryside then. When I moved out ten years later it was suburbia: an extension of the East End with people paying for their evenings out with dirty rolls of fivers from their back pockets, looking round all the time while they were counting them. Any day now, I thought, I'd have my old mate Casey as a next door neighbour.

From Chigwell I moved to a little village: and that's where I met the galloping Major. There's one thing you get to learn very quickly about village life: two things actually. One is that unless you're very careful you can get roped into just about everything going, from the church fair committee to the tug o'war team. The other is that you have to be awfully polite to people, while at the same time trying not to get involved too much. If you step out of line, there's always someone like the Major to make sure you know your place.

This bloke fancied himself as the village squire: a sort of master of foxhounds who'd lost his horse, his hounds and the fox. He used to swan around the village slapping his thigh with a riding crop, just like kids do when they're riding horses playing cowboys and Indians. My first brush with him (sorry, Basil) came because of Charley, my dog.

'Your dog barks,' he said to me one day when I was mowing the lawn.

'What d'you expect it to do? Whistle?'

He didn't take kindly to that at all.

'Your dog's barking is a nuisance. It's disturbing me. And my lady wife too.'

'I'm sorry, but the reason I've got a dog is 'cause it barks. That way I know there're people about who ain't supposed to be. He's no bloody good to me if he doesn't bark.'

'We'll talk about this again,' he said, doing a smart parade ground about-turn and whacking his thigh as he double-marched down the drive. Charley came out from behind a rhododendron bush and gave a low growl. The irony of it was that a couple of days later I discovered it wasn't my dog that was barking at all but some mastiff guard-dog in a house nearby. Not that this made any difference to the Major. He'd got it into his head that it was Charley who barked and there was no changing his mind. He even had a go about it to my father-in-law.

Vicki's dad had come down to look after the place while Vick and I were doing a Combined Services Entertainment tour of British bases, and this particular day he was doing a spot of gardening when the Major arrived on the scene.

'That man!' he bawled.

Whereupon Rob, who'd been an artillery sergeant in his time, sprang from his doubled-over weeding position and drew himself to attention. That was a big mistake, because now the Major knew he was dealing with an army man. Not only that – I'd put money on it that he probably knew his rank and regiment by the time he got up to him.

'That dog's causing a nuisance,' he told Rob, proceeding to walk round him, slapping his thigh and inspecting Rob's wellies. 'I don't want to have to tell you again.'

'No, sir,' says Rob. 'I'll see to it, sir.'

And mouths something else as the Major struts away.

Given that there was little Rob could do about Charley while I was away, and that Charley wasn't even the culprit, the situation remained the same until the Major did a rather foolish thing. He wrote me a letter, complaining about Charley, in which he suggested I was cruel to the dog. Not only was this untrue, my solicitor also said it could be taken as being libellous. So, being Christmas and all, I wrote him back a very nice letter, wishing him and the lady wife a merry Christmas and lots of cold turkey, and right at the end I added a little PS: 'As to your libellous allegations of cruelty, which my solicitor has informed me are apparent in your letter, I wish to inform you that I have sent a copy of it to the RSPCA in case they wish to investigate the matter further. Compliments of the season.'

That stopped him going on about the dog, but it didn't stop him poking his nose over the garden wall from time to time. That was enough for me to wind him up when the opportunity arose, which, by one of those beautiful little coincidences, it happened to.

Because I'm in the music business a lot of my friends are black, and a special friend is Madeleine Bell, who was in the Blue Mink pop group along with my old mate, Roger Cook. One Sunday Madeleine and her family came for a picnic, but they didn't just turn up in a car. Oh no. They rolled up in this great purple road coach that her husband of the

On safari in the village with Madeleine Bell.

time used to drive pop groups round in. Terrific, it was: showers, TV, kitchen, the full works. So while the rest of the village is going home from church, this purple monstrosity comes down the road, parks on the green outside the Major's and disgorges Madeleine and her husband, her cousin and husband plus their baby and another couple with a kid. All black and boogying across the green and up the Browns' drive. We had a nice day.

Next weekend I was looking round the village jumble sale, thinking I might find Vicki something for her birthday, when I saw this lovely Victorian handbag. Just the thing, I thought, and then discovered I didn't have any money on me. Fortunately the lady on the stall was the Major's wife, who was very nice about it.

'Don't worry,' she said. 'Pop over to my place this afternoon with the money.'

That's one of the advantages of living in the country. You'd never get that sort of treatment at Leather Lane market.

So later in the day I popped round with the money.

'Do come in,' said the lady. 'We're just having tea.'

Tiffin time, I thought. Jolly good. I spent a most pleasant half-hour. Lots of 'Thank you very much' and 'Don't mention it' as the tea and tiny cakes were passed around. I even remembered to pay for Vicki's handbag before leaving. I suppose I'd gone about twenty yards down the path when all of a sudden she called to me.

'By the way.' I took my hand off the gate and turned. 'We don't like darkies here, you know.'

I didn't say a word. To be honest I didn't know what to say. Anyway, it wasn't long afterwards that someone in the village came up to me and said, 'What's this I see in the paper about you selling your house to Cliff Richard?'

'Nothing in it,' I replied. 'You know what newspapers are like. Anything for a story.'

I forgot all about it until a week later when someone else said, 'I was in the village shop the other day and someone was saying you're selling your house to Cliff Richard.'

Whereupon the old tour brain started to click. So, it thinks, there's a little rumour going round, is there? Well, there's a wind-up here. Let's just think how we can get some percentage from it.

That evening in the local pub I picked the last guy in the village you'd choose to keep anything secret and just happened to ask if he'd heard I was selling my place to Cliff Richard.

'Between you and me, of course, it's nothing to do with Cliff Richard.'

'No?' he said, his eyes widening in expectation of something he hadn't heard yet.

'Not really. Cliff's involved, of course. You know he does all this work in Africa for the church, and some of the missionaries out there are in a bit of a bad way. Well, I believe he's buying it for them as some sort of rest home. You know, that sort of thing. I'm not much into it myself. It's all being handled by this African agency with Cliff putting up the money.'

I left it at that. Next thing I know the story's coming back to me from a different source: the woman who runs the village shop. So it's getting about.

'To be honest,' I tell her, leaning across the counter so no one else in the shop can hear, 'I'm a bit worried about it. I've heard from some mates of mine in the business that he wants to turn it into an open-air borstal for deprived colonial kids. Trouble is he's offering me such a good price that I can't afford not to sell.'

So saying I picked up my coffee beans and left them all to it. I don't think the day was out before the Major strolled up the drive with a cheerful wave, leant down and rubbed Charley behind the ears.

'Lovely place you have here, Joe.' And with a little confidential lowering of the voice as between two old campaign mates. 'Not thinking of leaving us, are you?'

I was already waiting for it.

32 For Queen and country

I suppose it was too good a chance to miss. After all, it's not every day that someone offers to buy your wife. The trouble was that this guy was serious – and when I agreed to part with Vicki for a suitable remuneration, I wasn't.

The problem arose on one of the tours I was doing for Combined Services Entertainment. (They're called CSE for short, which is quite useful, because when people start going on about their A-levels and O-levels, I can say I've got four CSEs to my name.) The CSEs are more or less an extension of ENSA (Entertainments National Services Association): little groups of entertainers touring round the outposts of the Empire to put on a show for the chaps and the lads. There aren't many lasses about, which is why Vicki and any other girls on the tour got the five-star VIP treatment. The trips were great fun. Not big earners but a good boost for the ego to appear before an audience starved of live entertainment and some faces from home.

We'd all meet up at Brize Norton, and the RAF would fly us off to places like Gibraltar, Cyprus, Malta, Oman and Gan. I thought Gan was terrific: very hot, being just a few degrees south of the equator, and with some of the best scuba diving I've come across – lovely coral reefs and all kinds of underwater life. Whereas in Salalah, in Oman, the only diving we did was for cover when some restless natives began lobbing mortars in our direction. We should have had campaign medals for that tour.

That was one thing about the CSE tours. They never lacked variety. One night you'd be in the petty officers' mess somewhere, knocking back rum and swapping yarns in the saltiest language; next night you

The Gan Sub-aqua Club.

might be in dinner jacket and black bow tie toasting the Queen with vintage port which had just been piped in to the officers' mess. Some places we visited, the different messes would hold a raffle to see who would have the honour of being host to the various artists. I loved it.

The concerts themselves were nearly always open-air affairs: usually a stage with a concrete canopy over it and then nothing but sand or wilderness. One place we played, it was ever so funny. Everyone brought their own seating, except for the officers who had their servants carry out the armchairs from the officers' mess. Then they were all arranged in military pecking order. Officers in the front three rows, all in full uniform, plus their invited guests: behind them the NCOs, and behind them the other ranks. Right at the back stood the locals.

Halfway through the show there was an incredible crash of thunder and the heavens opened. I'd seen rain before but this was something else. Out front people were running for cover as if their very lives depended on it. But not the front three rows. Oh no. They sat there through the downpour, politely applauding every act as if it were an evening out at Covent Garden. And funniest of all, when the rain eased and you could actually see farther than the front few rows, dotted here and there among the empty seats were the crawlers: the promotion hopefuls who weren't going to risk losing the chance of another stripe because of a thunderstorm.

Two things made a big impression on me during those trips: one was the way the British officers lived and behaved; the other was the conditions in which the locals lived. Sometimes, being entertained in the mess, you'd think you'd stepped into the pages of a book about the Raj. On Masirah, a desert island off the coast of Oman, they even had their own golf course. It was like one big bunker, because when I say this was a desert island, I mean desert. The only bit of green was a pot-plant in the officers' mess. The rest of the place was sand and nothing but sand. For the greens on the golf course they packed the sand solid with water. Only they weren't called greens – they were called browns and looked after by a brown-keeper. Just for the record, the ball was red.

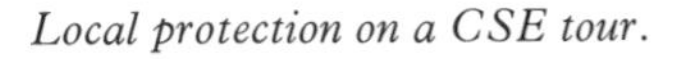
Local protection on a CSE tour.

The other side of the coin was Drum City, where most of the local population lived in oil drums, bits of shelter made from corrugated iron, and squalor. The average lifespan of a male was thirty years; females were lucky if they got past babyhood because the custom was to throw any girl baby on the roof of the shack, and if she survived the family would keep her. If twins were born, the healthy one would be kept and the other one was thrown on the roof to die. The staple local diet was fish, unless you were a donkey, in which case you ate the cardboard boxes that were thrown out at the British base.

The reason for the squalid housing, so the story went, was that the local sheik had banned any building on the island for a hundred years, following a massacre late last century. The islanders had all gathered on the shore to greet a boatload of Portuguese sailors coming in for water, or whatever, but one of the sailors had panicked and shot an islander. This upset them a bit, what with them having come down as a welcoming party, so they set about the Portuguese with sawfish blades – nasty things, about four feet long with enormous jagged teeth. Not to put too fine a point on it, they did for the lot of them. Very naughty, decreed the local sheik, and as a punishment, no building was permitted on the island for a hundred years. The ban didn't apply to the British, who built a base and a hospital, and it was in one of the hospital wards that Vicki and I were quartered when we went there.

One morning I came out to see a long line of locals stretching from the hospital compound out into the desert. Women mostly, wearing yashmaks and carrying children, all just standing and waiting.

'What's all this?' I asked the Medical Officer when I got to the mess.

'I run a clinic every week for them. Bit against the rules, but we try to do something.'

'What sort of things do the locals suffer from?'

'The lot. You've seen how they live. Hopeless, eh? Tell the truth, if it's above the waist I give 'em aspirin. If it's below the waist I give 'em something for syphilis. I had one chap in a while back – "Devils in the head", he said. Better give him two aspirin, I thought. He came back the following week with these two aspirin taped to his forehead. Full of smiles. The devils had gone.'

The mess servant brought us some more coffee.

'How come that bloke speaks with a Geordie accent?' I asked.

'That's Newcastle,' replied the MO. 'He learnt his English when there was a Newcastle regiment stationed here some years ago.'

'He's a big man around here,' said another officer opposite.

'How come?' I asked.

'Oh, this and that. He's a dealer for one thing.'

Just then an orderly came in to say that one of the women by the compound had collapsed, so the MO knocked back his coffee and I followed him outside. By English life it was still early, but already it was boiling hot and there were flies everywhere. It was the sort of place where they give you a drink and a beer mat, but you don't put the glass on the beer mat; you put the beer mat on the glass to keep the flies away. I quickly forgot about Newcastle. Until lunch.

I could see old Newcastle giving Vicki the eye. Actually he wasn't that old: only thirty-three but he looked all of sixty-five. We were all sitting there eating; he was serving the food, and I could see he wanted to say something to me. But I was always talking. Eventually he caught me with my mouth full.

'Har mooch d'yer want fer yer missus, marra?'

I swallowed. Had I heard this bloke correctly?

'You want to buy my wife?' I asked.

Newcastle beamed and nodded.

'Take her away, mate,' I told him. 'She's all yours.'

Just then I felt a kick on my shins not from Vicki (who obviously fancied a bit of Newcastle Brown) but from the MO, who was sitting on the other side of me. At the same time he was waving his hand at Newcastle and telling him to bugger off.

'What's the matter?' I asked.

'You know I told you earlier that Newcastle was a dealer? Well, what I didn't get round to telling you was that he's a dealer in wives. A wife-dealer. Just the other week, so I heard, he sold his twelve-year-old wife for £200, bought another wife to replace her, and with the change he got himself a little motorbike. That's why he's the big man around these parts.'

Vicki and I both laughed.

'You're having us on, mate,' I said. 'This is 1979.'

'No, I'm serious. And so was Newcastle.'

He was, too. For the next day or so he kept pestering me. Wherever I was, there he was. It was like the old joke: psssst, mister, wanna sell your wife? Only it got beyond a joke.

'What am I going to do about this bloke?' I asked the MO. 'He's driving me bananas.'

'There's only one way out of it. You'll have to outbid him.'

So I did. We settled down to business, me and Newcastle.

'How much are you willing to pay me, Newcastle? Bearing in mind she's been on television.'

Newcastle shook and scratched his head. Television didn't cut much ice on a desert island. Other considerations were more important. Such as:

'How old is she?'

'Over thirty,' I said, trying to be as fair to Vick as possible.

Newcastle pulled an awful face and looked troubled. And I hadn't told him she'd had two kids yet.

'Thirty pounds,' he offered.

I shook my head. Not enough.

'And this ring,' he added, taking from his finger a large gold ring which would have fetched all of a fiver in Petticoat Lane.

'Sorry, mate. You'll have to do better than that.'

Newcastle scratched his chin.

'Just fer you, man, I'll send my best donkey to pick her up.'

I had to laugh then. The guy was so serious and the whole situation was so ludicrously funny. All the same, I never let Vicki out of my sight till we were off the island.

33 Just another gig

The phone rang.

'I know it's short notice, Joe,' said the promoter, 'and you're not supposed to be on till ten. But do you think you could go on at nine o'clock?'

'All right by me,' I replied. I always like to get on early because, to start with, the audience haven't had too much to drink, and that's an advantage as far as cabaret is concerned – it means they're more inclined to listen. Also, it's nice to get home that little bit earlier. 'Give me ten minutes to get hold of the band and I'll come back to you.'

'No problem,' said the lads; all except Roger, the guitar player. He wasn't answering.

'He's probably on his way,' said Vicki. 'You know what he's like. Always early.'

I thought she was no doubt right and let the promoter know it was fine for nine. However, I hadn't reckoned on what the traffic reports refer to as 'the elevated section of the M4'.

Living where I do, that's the problem with gigs to the east of London. It's almost the same distance from the centre of town as it is from home to the centre. In mileage it's nothing, but with the traffic situation so unpredictable around London, the time it takes getting across town could be better employed getting to John O'Groats. It wouldn't be so bad if they gave you some warning, but in this country you're slap in the middle of a traffic jam – and unable to get out of it – by the time you see the notice advising you of roadworks ahead and suggesting you take an alternative route.

Same with the radio. There's nothing more frustrating than sitting

The Brown family.

in the car, with the traffic stretching out miles in front of you and building up steadily behind you, hearing some cheeky DJ saying 'If you're heading east on the M4, try to avoid the elevated section'. You can't help wondering if he knew about it earlier but decided to put on three or four consecutive Stevie Wonder tracks while he went for a piss. Just think: if he hadn't had a weak bladder, you could have come off at the previous junction.

Consequently, if I'm driving east, I make sure I leave home in plenty of time. As I did this particular Friday night. But after cruising along happily for an hour – complete standstill. I switched on Capital Radio for a traffic report. In front of us people were getting out of their cars and stretching their legs. One bloke, with a carful of kids and a rubber dinghy on his roof-rack, was breaking out sandwiches and shouting at his wife because he couldn't get the top off their thermos flask. And then it came over the radio.

'There we had a few tracks from Stevie Wonder's latest album: and doesn't that guy really get things moving.'

Pity he's not here, I thought.

'Now here's a traffic flash just in. If you're travelling east on the M4, try to avoid the elevated section because – ha ha ha ha, you're never going to believe this – a herd of wild horses has broken loose from a field and they're running amok along the eastbound carriageway. One for Clint Eastwood there. Meanwhile, stay cool, folks, and here's Barry Manilow.'

Talk about adding insult to injury. If there's one thing I hate more than being late, it's Barry bleedin' Manilow.

Then the police arrived. A jam sandwich went hurtling down the hard shoulder on our left, and after a few minutes two coppers came weaving in and out among the cars on their German motorbikes – another insult to injury if you ask me. All went quiet again. Till the guy up front finally got the top off the thermos flask and let out a howl of anger and pain as he doused his crotch in boiling tea. Twenty minutes later we spotted the wild horses. One came galloping right past us, hotly pursued by a red-faced police sergeant, running like the devil, clutching a tuft of grass in his hand and shouting 'Nice gee gee. Nice grass, gee gee.' Some hope. Horse and perspiring policeman disappeared in the general direction of Reading, and after another half hour we got moving again.

I arrived at the gig an hour late. That is to say, I arrived an hour late for the original time of ten o'clock. The promoter was going bananas.

'What happened?' he screamed. 'Where have you been? They're going mad out there.'

I opened my mouth to tell him about the herd of wild horses but settled on my sister-in-law having a miscarriage and me having to take her to the hospital. His jaw clamped shut. He tried a sympathetic smile through clenched teeth and said with some effort as he backed stiffly out of the dressing-room:

'Oh, I'm sorry to hear that. Could you get ready to go on as soon as possible, please?'

I heard him curse and clatter down the corridor to try to calm his now foot-stamping clientèle. Vicki went in search of the ladies' loo to change in and I looked around at the band. Everyone was there except the guitar player.

'Where's Roger?' I asked.

'He can't come,' answered the Bass Player. 'His sister-in-law's had a miscarriage and he's had to take her to hospital. Straight up.'

'Does he know that?' I asked, pointing in the direction the promoter had gone.

'He took the phone call.'

Not a good start.

'OK, lads. Get on stage and make like something's going to happen while I get changed. You'll have to do the play-on without Roger. Once I'm on I'll do his solos.'

I struggled into my stage gear and made what I thought was a dignified entrance. The keyboard player was doing his best to cope with a riff that was really suitable only for an electric guitar, several of which had been placed on a stand near the drum kit. I grabbed one and felt in my pocket for a plectrum. Absolutely essential. Except that I didn't have one. Not that it mattered. Making my dignified entrance, I'd tripped over the mains-lead to my amp and ripped the wires from the plug. It was going to be one of those gigs.

We struggled through the first song while one of the roadies loped low across the stage behind me to fix the amplifier. Quite why they always stoop low to look inconspicuous I'll never know. If anything it makes them even more obvious. The opening number out of the way –

On the set of the TV show Unforgettable.

I was relieved to notice Vicki hadn't got herself locked in the loo – I tried to collect my wits and chat to the audience.

'I really am sorry I'm late,' I began. 'My car broke down.'

'Car!' yelled some aggressive woman at the back. 'Some of us 'ave got bleedin' buses to catch.'

Mistake number one: never apologize to a hostile audience. There was only one thing for it – total honesty. I told them about the wild horses on the M4 and made it as funny as possible. By the time I got to the police sergeant, he'd been promoted to inspector and the horse was eating his cap. I could feel them warming to me, all except one woman slightly to my left who sat staring straight in front of her.

At last my amplifier came to life and the roadie scuttled off the stage behind me. Right, now I was in control. We went straight into 'A Picture of You' and they applauded the introduction. Got them, I thought, and when we finished the song we got a good reaction, apart from the lady in front who still stared morosely in front of her.

The next song was a very simple instrumental version of 'All Things Bright and Beautiful'. Ever since I first recorded this in the early sixties, I've included it in my act. For one thing I like its simplicity, but I've also found that it's a wonderful yardstick to measure the attentiveness of an audience. I can gauge the whole outcome of the act from the reaction to this one song. I play it very quietly on an acoustic guitar into a microphone, and usually you can hear a pin drop.

I picked up the guitar and began. Dink dink dink donk dink, dink-dink. The audience hushed. I'm on my way home, I thought. But just as I got to where the words would have been 'Each little flower that opens, Each little bird that sings', there was the most horrendous screeching, like a whole flock of birds being boiled in oil. The mood was broken: people clapped their hands to their ears as two thousand watts of what is known as feedback came screaming out of the speakers. One old bloke in the front shot to his feet as if he was having a fit, frantically fumbling at his shirt front as he tried to turn down his hearing aid. In the end he ripped the wires right out and crashed back into his seat as if he'd been shot. He was as pale as a ghost.

On stage roadies were scuttling everywhere, all stooping low to avoid detection. Suddenly everything went deathly quiet – someone had pulled the mains plug. I tried to speak and it all happened again. Someone had pushed the mains plug. This time, however, the sound was different. A low, ominous hum, so vibrant that it made the glasses on the tables clink together. Little bits of plaster fell off the ceiling. I was at a loss what to do. I signalled desperately to one of the lads to pull the plug again. The noise stopped. Everything stopped. I stood there on stage in front of a shell-shocked audience. Someone started to clap ironically, and the roadie who'd pulled the plug had the cheek to stand up from his crouching position and take a bow. You bastard, I thought. I'll have you afterwards.

Once again I'd lost the audience, so this time I did what I felt was natural. I left the stage and walked down among them, going round the tables cracking gags I didn't even know I knew, all the time watching the crew trying to find the fault in the PA system. I was beginning to sweat. My brain was racing with panic because I knew I couldn't get away with it for much longer. Out of the corner of my eye I saw the roadie put the mains plug back in and switch on the system. I said a quick prayer and felt rather than heard the PA come back to life. I had another chance.

The crowd, I felt, was still with me, apart from the woman in the front who continued to stare straight in front of her. Oh well, you can't win 'em all. I walked back to the steps leading to the stage and stood at the bottom, by the front row of tables.

'Ladies and gentlemen,' I began, 'I do appreciate your patience with us, but it's your own fault for coming to see such a polished act.'

They laughed and I relaxed a little. I felt grateful really. My confidence returned. 'After all this it's nice to see so many smiling faces.'

Then I made the mistake of my life. I indicated with an outstretched hand the lady in front who was sitting just to my left about five feet away.

'All except this one here. She hasn't looked at me all night.'

Immediately the man sitting next to her rose to his feet and slapped something hard into my open hand. My fingers closed automatically around it and he let go of his end. I looked. It was a long white stick.

'That's because she's blind,' he said.

The entire audience heard him. I stood there, stunned, holding the stick. I don't know what made me say what I said next, and to this day I don't know how I got away with it. It was almost as if it was the ghost of Jimmy Wheeler speaking.

'Listen, Mrs,' I heard my own alien voice say. 'If he's got these bloody microphones fixed properly you'll soon be bleedin' deaf as well.'

There were gasps from the audience, followed by a shocked, embarrassed silence. Then the blind lady turned in the direction of my voice and burst out laughing. It was the most wonderful sound, and everybody laughed with her. It's marvellous how ordinary folk will support you when they know you're having a bad time. That's one of the things I do like about this business.